Lewis Anston's

ON THE BRIDGE

An autistic story

On the Bridge – An autistic story

Copyright © 2024 Lewis Anston
Published by Verify, Inc.
ISBN: 979-8-883-64088-8
Library of Congress Control Number: 2024920489

All rights reserved. No part of this publication may be reproduced, stored in a retrieval system, or transmitted in any form or by any means–electronic, mechanical, photocopying, recording, or otherwise–without the prior written permission of the publisher and copyright owners.

Cover photo Copyright © 2024: Erika Rashka Watercolors and illustration; Anabel Schk Fonts and Layout.

# ACKNOWLEDGEMENT

I want to thank the people who encouraged me to write this book through the insufferable lockdown era of six feet distance, while either paper- or cloth-masks covered our mouths and noses.

As a coping mechanism and preventing myself from being driven insane I wrote this book about me being a neurodivergent in a typical world. This book possibly could help not just me but all neurodivergent people; the only goal for this book is to feel seen and be heard.

I would love to thank my Mom who has been there for me from the very beginning. She ran from doctor to doctor to get a diagnosis and help. She pored over books and journals to find out how my situation could be improved. She had me started on individual educational plans (IEPs) when first available and she didn't miss a single meeting.

I would love to thank my grandmother and my aunt from the sea of people that support me especially because they were the real reason why I turned those words from the cabinets of my brain onto the laptop of a *Google* Doc, feverishly typing like I'm Jim Carrey in "Bruce Almighty" typing out recalled experiences from my own life over the years with the names and locations changed for the safety and the protection of others and myself included.

I would also like to thank my Dad and my

siblings and the rest of my family and friends who are always there and support me.

I also would like to thank Eve Pines who spent hours with me on editing this book, which is so very much appreciated.

If I could "count the scars, there's a moment of truth," because "that there wouldn't be this," point to this book "if there hadn't been you." (Quotation from the Taylor Swift song "thanK you aIMee")

# PREFACE

When the British clarity group "National Autism Association" first was founded in 1962, they used the puzzle piece in their logo to give an idea that autism is *just a puzzling discovery.* Sure, at the time in the early sixties, autism was historical, and a puzzling discovery and the logo had a meaning within the heart and core of the autism community. Over time, the National Autism Association rebranded themselves with the start of a new, colorful logo that seems to demystify autism as a whole, instead of making it just a blue puzzle and autism an alienating, terrible thing.

I'm also sure that when autism first was discovered it was not thoroughly looked at as a concept and research was lacking. Scientists and doctors at the time thought when a child was diagnosed with autism that it had something to do with a child's own emotional and social problems.

Somewhere in the late nineties, the role of behavioral therapy and crazy treatments to help curb autism were developed but they were battling it like it was a cancer. Battling it because they couldn't even be bothered to learn something new about it and try to demystify, emerge and embrace what it means to be autistic; instead, they demonized autism like it is a burden.

I want them to take something that seems

super puzzling and utilize it, partake to something good, unique and impactful.

Here is my story.

To the readers out there, this is a story, providing my viewpoint of me, a non-neurotypical person. I have autism, high-functioning autism to be exact (also called neurodivergent; trying to keep track of what to call me; someone on the spectrum).

From the get-go in my life, I didn't know that I have autism and now in my early twenties, I begin to realize that back then I was very reserved, within myself, and only now can I explain my own behavior and personality and why I'm the way I am and who I am today.

I've learned that people often think people with autism are unalike and mismatched among society, or at least we are treated like we are mismatched in a crowd of other people. I'm not saying that you need to feel sorry for me and the people on the autism spectrum. But maybe have the patience to listen, instead of tapping on an imaginary watch, impatiently.

I'm only writing, telling, presenting a story and nothing else. Not to set my records straight, just to tell it in my own unique voice. And maybe one of the other autistic folks can see themselves in my story.

I'm the Director, the Producer, and the

Protagonist of my life.

I'm the lead character in that respect, with that perspective. This book is not your typical memoir, but I hope you can stick with it.

This is my story . . .

## PART I - COMING OF AGE

"You're italic, I'm in bold / Call me cocky, watch your tone / You better love me, 'cause you're just a clone." ~ Song "Copycat" by Billie Ellish

This is from me and from my voice.

## CHAPTER 01 – BIRTH

*"I often wake up in the morning feeling a kind of pressure to mask out my own autism in order to fit into the puzzle peg of a star that society intends on fitting me into in which I could be a circle peg."* – Lewis Anston, Author

"Being autistic is so daringly beautiful and refreshing in the way my brain works," is not something I would say. The amount of work 'I've put in because of the way I am, to adjust to a world designed for neurotypicals, is very exhausting. I try to mimic the "normal" people in order to feel like I belong and be able to fit in, but that constant "keeping up" often causes me to feel burnt out.

To make things work for me in a neurotypical world, I have to work much harder than someone who doesn't have autism. I don't need a cake, a party hat and confetti to celebrate a pity party; all I ever need is a phone, a computer, a megaphone, a voice, a brain, a free-spirit mind, love, and to be shown, to be heard, and to be seen, in identify-first, first-person narrations… and some patience and to be listened to and understood.

I've learned that happiness isn't something to be granted in the morning the moment you wake up;

instead, each day there are going to be setbacks that'll sucker punch you. So, I have learned that we can't always live in some alternative universe where other emotions are discarded but happiness is being put on a pedestal.

"You should be happy, you have everything you need; food, clothing, a roof over your head," is what I'm told. But there are so many more emotions I feel other than happiness.

People in my life mean well. They want to coach me, train me, work with me, often until a limit is reached. Knowing your limits is as important as knowing your worth, especially being autistic. I totally get and understand that everyone wants to help but I can quickly reach my limits. Breaching my limits causes an overload, and I have to stop what I'm doing; so, I take a break, surf the web, listen to music, walk around the front or back yard of my family's house and slowly start again; re-energize.

Let's normalize allowing people with autism to ease into situations or give them breaks rather than not having patience or worse tossing them into the autism soup with "he'll never learn, he's autistic."

"Once you've accepted your flaws, no one can use them against you." said Tyrion Lannister, from Game of Thrones. Well, I've accepted that I'm autistic, and I don't want people to use it against me, but sometimes they do. Hear me out. Here are some of my life's anecdotes.

\*\*\*

My mom, Olivia, had me when she was eighteen, then just a freshman in college. She called my grandma, Anna, to tell her that she was pregnant, and she needed her help.

Imagine a mother hearing that her teenage daughter is expecting at that age – horrifying – I overheard my grandma tell the story that she was near steps when that call came in and became dizzy, when Olivia uttered those words, and my grandma grabbed on to the railing, because as she explained later for a young mother like that the trajectory of her life will change immediately and forever.

*What would the future hold?* We know the statistics, "Less than 2 percent of teen moms who have a baby before they turn 18 earn a college degree by the time they're 30."

A new mother has to rearrange her life like her own room for another human being to live with. It's scary for teenage girls to be pregnant because they are themselves still children. Their lives and focus change drastically in order to make their child's life satisfying.

Of all the different options her mom, dad, aunts and uncles threw at her, my mom insisted on having me. She told her mom in tears, "I want to have my baby, I don't care if I'm only 18."

"Alright," my grandma said, "best for you to then move back home until you have the baby and then continue your college."

That was that. We moved back in with my grandma.

The birth was rough, somehow, I got stuck in the birth canal, it was something about how my mom's birth canal was formed; I'm not saying my mom is deformed just that the canal was shaped unusually, leaving me with a small hole in my head. Apparently the fetal scalp electrode was stabbing against my head while I was stuck in the birth canal and being pushed out.

My mom labored in excruciating pain all night with my grandma helplessly looking on. Well, the birth might not have been straight forward, but after all the turmoil there was a happy ending.

I was born one nice late summer Monday, in Fairfax Hospital, in Virginia.

My thirty-eight-year-old grandma stayed with me and my mom the entire time, and she tells stories of a nurse walking into the delivery room right after I was born and shouting, "Oh no, mama, you can't be walking around yet, back in that bed." She assumed my grandmother was my mother, something that would continue to happen.

My grandma pointed to the bed where my mom was laying, "No, you want her!"

The doctors decided I needed to stay at the

hospital to prevent an infection, and let the hole in my head heal. My grandma and mom stayed with me another day – the insurance wouldn't cover more - and my mom was using the restroom when the doctor from the new shift came in and asked my grandma, "how are you feeling?"

Grandma famously said, "Just a bit nauseous," and then explained that the new mom will be right back.

After two weeks of medication to control an infection on my head I finally got to go home to live with my grandma, mom, and aunt Ingrid who was three years old.

Now I've always heard stories about the times when I was a baby and times as a toddler from both my mom, my aunt and my grandma.

Around the time when I was a toddler, my mom was either at school, or studying or with friends, just like any eighteen-year-old, leaving my grandma to raise me and Ingrid.

As the matriarch of the family, grandma was that one strong pillar, the one thing upright to keep the foundation steady and standing. My mom was busy with school and studying, my biological father – not from the lack of my mom trying and many tearful phone calls later - didn't want to have anything to do with me, but the one standing vertically strong remained. That is the definition of my grandma, she is like a pillar holding up the heavy foundation of our then little family. She helped my mom raise me by filling in for her when needed and providing health insurance for us, making her my shared legal guardian.

When I first realized that, it got me thinking that the definition of our family really is to be close-knit, always-have-your-back type, and I realized that people in our family worry about each other for the best reasons and intentions. Families are groups of people who happen to be related to each other and worry about every little crack and crevice, like we're all Marvin in "Finding Nemo." That's what families really are, and they support great aspirations and create true raw real happiness. I do also believe if I didn't have someone like my grandma to step up in getting my mom and I health insurance, I would be a whole different person than I'm today.

I learned early on that it took a long while for me to walk. In the months after I was first born at the turn of the twenty-first century, a doctor named Dr. Ophelia Whick misdiagnosed me, thinking I would not be an intellectual individual, explaining I would not be able to talk, walk, see, or think like a *normal* human being.

But I proved her wrong.

My grandma told me that one day, little me was sitting like all thirty months old babies do, turning my little head, catching a glimpse of a mirror, catching my own reflection. Almost like that reflection sparked something within my small body, a type of curiosity. Seeing myself in the polished metal wasn't the tip of the iceberg, it was the solution to any of the limitations of my misdiagnosis. I pulled myself up on the mirror and walked along it. I was like a Disney character, grew so fascinated by the reflection of myself bouncing off from a reflective object on a wall. Let's say I was across the room and seeing myself, my reflection, filled me up with glee like a fuel tank. I wanted a closer look. I scooted and slowly pulled myself up on the mirror. My grandmother was on the other side of the room, seeing my very first step and screamed with glee, embracing my first step. She was in awe that I started walking at age two-in-a-half. She called my mom who was at her college bookstore job working her way through college, and at that the time my mom believed the doctors' diagnosis of mine by heart and by truth, never expecting me to walk, after all I was going on 3.

"He's walking, he's walking!!" My grandmother said over and over into phone.
"I don't believe you," was my mom's initial reaction. Mind you, there weren't cell phone cameras where you could take a video of every second of your life.
"He is! He's REALLY walking!!" My

grandma insisted.

My mom dropped everything and moments later came home to see her son's first steps for herself, while I had to prove that I could really muster the second round of my first steps. It was like the scene in *The Simpsons Movie* when Marge sees Maggie out of the dome, but Homer insists, she's 'right here' in the sandbox. But, while they both resumed their daily routines, what appeared in Maggie's sandbox was a sinkhole. So, I had my sinkhole moment. When my mom was in the same room with my grandmother and myself, it was like me being put on a stage with a bright, beaming spotlight shining on me. Silence and a man's coughing and me still not stepping up.

My mom was disappointed, "He's not walking. Are you sure you didn't imagine it?"

"No, no, he was a moment ago." My grandmother insisted. Moments after while they were having a semi-argument, I leaped into that sinkhole, beginning to prop myself up with the help of my own reflection in that grandiose mirror. Almost like I was Jess in *New Girl* where she jazz-handedly sang to the song, *Surrender* to divulge the tension of her struggling married parents. The debate stopped abruptly, seeing me propped up and I turned to the direction of that mirror and began to again take little, baby steps (no puns intended) towards it.

My mom thought she was in a dream, but no,

it was happening. Her own son was walking at the age of two-and-a-half, unlike what the doctor had said "never." A mix of emotions of elation and disappointment of not being the one to see my very, very first step at that moment, but also proud of her son always, of me taking my first steps, and not missing that milestone of a not-so-average child. I did it anyway and from then on, we let no misdiagnosis turn against me or limit me. Like that TLC song where you don't go chasing waterfalls, I do the opposite. My misdiagnosis could be saying to me 'don't go outgrowing limitations,' I do it anyway.

That first step, that boldness brought great strides for me, a little sliver of independence and resistance to myself. If a limitation or a wall tries to form in front or around me, I take a metaphorical sledgehammer and smash it to smithereens.

My family told me that my speech was delayed and after multiple ear infections, at the age of three one of the ENTs recommended ear tubes. During surgery they discovered that most of my young life I had been living with liquid in my ears. No wonder my speech was delayed! I wasn't able to hear well, and like a deaf person couldn't learn speech by mimicking others.

After the surgery, I had a lot of catching up to do. My grandma tells me I asked a lot of questions that only my mom, grandma and aunt could understand. "I want a 'marshmallow?" I called it "macamow" or my grandma said I had many questions "what is this..," or "what would you do if/when...," in words only my family would understand, and even though my mom or aunt or grandma would answer, I would repeat the same questions as if the answers weren't satisfactory or I wanted to hear them again and again or maybe they just didn't stick. I had a never-ending set of them.

At the age of five, my grandma, tired of me asking the same questions over and over showed me how to use *Google*, how to put the words together and how to type. I used my pointer-fingers to type one letter at a time, sometimes even mistyping the words, but my grandma showed me how to get my answers eventually. The computer never tired of me asking the same thing over and over again. Thank goodness for *Google*, my grandma claims, my typing the words and finding the answers was the most informative thing that helped my brain grow and expand.

Still, my mom took me to many doctor's appointments, many checkups; different evaluations; eager to find a solution and diagnosis for my "developmental delays."

To the utmost, I now understand the hardships of what family endure and what it truly means to be a family, rather than seeing 'happy' family pictures on Facebook that only create images that are too perfect, almost plastic. A truly happy, close-knit family is better than families who are under peer pressure from other families to be better than the rest and do it for the wrong reasons. Our family only wants everyone to be the best they can be with the best intentions for growth, safety, comfort, and sometimes tough love.

# CHAPTER 02 - EARLY CHILDHOOD

It brings me a different type of joy to look at my own photo album showing pictures of myself as a preschool kid. Not that I'm like Peter Pan who's in Neverland, not wanting to grow up to be an adult. It's a very different case from how I feel about that. I admire how happy I was back then in those pictures, and I try to recapture that happiness in my adulthood without even re-experiencing my whole childhood altogether.

Looking at baby photos and pictures of me that little just to admire and re-capture that same feeling that I once had as a kid, innocent, free, re-imagining how happiness occurred back then and how it feels now so very differently as an adult.

As a kid I didn't really know that I had autism, leaving me blissfully unaware of who I really was. Now, looking at my old childhood photos I try to imagine in order to have a better idea of why I was always so smiley and what made me smile that wide, a smile that today is so hard to recreate.

*Why was I this happy? What led to my own happiness or brought on so much joy? Unawareness? Oblivion? Uninformed then about the surrounding world in which my own realities intertwined?* Maybe I was only a kid living his life, unapologetically. I was without any form of social media unlike the kids of nowadays. It was different from their day-to-day lives. I didn't have the stress of being represented on the screen of a phone, posing in a certain way instructed by a parent. I had a childhood of playing outside or just chilling inside, appearing delightfully bored on the outside but inside my own little mind I had and continue to have a unique, interesting imagination. An imagination that made me more of an introvert and kept me reticent. I talked to myself as if I have a secret friendship with my own self, because of how different I felt.

    Yes, I say now that I felt different growing up but back then I didn't know how to translate that into my own words. It's like a totally different language. More on that next.

    I did say that I have a unique imagination which made me feel more isolated from other kids around me, like propping me in a corner of a classroom, not ever to be seen. The kind of imagination where certain images I see, like a movie poster of some kind, make me feel like the images in that poster are watching, following in my footsteps. I know that it is silly and unrealistic to think the people in a plain poster of some movies are following me or can make me shudder, some in fear and some in fascination. But in every movement or any silly, funny facial expressions in the movie poster, my head gives a reaction to each nuance. It's a bit of a weird fixation though and I'm known to having set up multiple DVD boxes of movies in front of me every time I watch TV, as if I've made friends. The covers fascinated me and kept me busy for hours.

      I'm too much of an introvert and I can't throw myself out there to make friends my own age. Because I was so reserved, I didn't know how it would even be possible to make friends my own age, because I was too much in my own mind. That's probably why when I was in the preschool and elementary SACC (the School Aged Child Care) programs I had the experiences I had.

      Already when I was a preschooler at the Little Sunshine Ray, the teasing started. You want to know what? I have a very vivid memory of something that happened a long time ago, the kind that makes me wince and cringe in embarrassment of who I once was. It includes a vivid imagination where I could recall imagining myself on a stage dancing to a Janet Jackson song *All for You*. And all of a sudden, I realized even those smiles in the photos came with challenges.

~

      I can remember a story at the Little Sunshine Ray Daycare where I was a young, little champ in the sandbox being in my own imagination, away from the other kids. I imagined being in the space program heading to the Moon or Mars and then not having to talk to other kids, as I played in the sandbox. I was fairly prone to fits and tantrums when another child breached my imaginary line in the sand where I was sitting. I didn't have the proper vocabulary to say something like 'go away,' I just simply threw my arms around like I'm the little bald kid in a children show called Caillou fussing up, because I didn't know how to express myself through words. It was hard being that kid in the sandbox who was so uncommunicative and wanted to say 'go away' but the gap of my throat wouldn't cross that void. Now looking back not knowing it then, I feel bad, or even sad about what type of kid I was. Shy, uncommunicative, quiet, with a big imagination, a world of my own I created at just the tender age of a preschooler, when I couldn't even imagine making friends with another kid my own age.

  One day, our pre-school teacher arranged a celebration; a Luau-themed party and picture this: me as a young, shy, timid little chap playing a charade that had gone a bit southwest, not south, but southwest.

  That day I distinctively remember playing my turn on a game of charade, which was a stretch to my comfort zone. Like, if this were a *Friends* episode, it would be titled *The One in The Sandbox*, because that stretch of me extending my little bubble in playing a game with other kids was like sending out

Morse code to others. I didn't really know how to play charades at the time but knew from me playing in that sandbox with my imagination how to act out an animal, something easy for kids to know and be able to guess with no problem. So, I did act out an animal: I flung out my hands, flapping my imaginary wings; I tried to master it but sort of butchered it and how I was doing it made the kids shriek with laughter.

 Don't get me wrong, my present self would love the attention of them laughing with me, but my younger self surely did not understand why they were laughing and thought they were laughing at me. But I didn't really know immediately, so I just rolled with the punches, rolled along with it, kept swinging my arms up and down, and was almost as fascinating as a celebrity who posted a funny video. I continued to play out other animals and each time I acted out another one, the laughter became shriller.

 There were no teachers in sight, maybe getting all the party supplies they had in storage, gearing up for the little celebration all had planned. No one was in sight to back me up or calm the kids, and now the laughter was so excessive and felt so very ear-splitting that my little preschool ears could not bear it. The only defense mechanism I had in store for me was to find the nearest beanbag chair and hide behind it. I pressed my hands to my ears, tried to say stop in a hoarse voice I did not recognize, the high-pitched laughter grew even worse, and it threw me into an out-of-control state that I wanted to do nothing but cry and disappear. I tried it again this time more firmly: "Stop it! Stop laughing! Stop! Stop! Stop!" The more I said 'stop' the more the howling grew, it was as piercing as when an opera singer sings above 100 decibels, or like Mariah Carey hitting that highest note in her song *Emotions*, times twenty kids. At this point, this hopeless point, to me it felt like it was never ending in my own little brain which only I felt pain.

Finally, after what felt like days of never-ending shrills, my knight-in-shiny-armor came into the classroom with all the party gear, and quickly threw the decorations down on a table.

"Children!" she hollered, stunned about what she was seeing. She quickly sized up the situation and from her point of view it was me hiding behind a beanbag like a scared meerkat nearly frozen stiff and the other kids sitting so close to each other, still laughing and pointing.

"Children!" she said again, the mob was so riled up. She took a deep breath, and frowned. "Now," She started to say, "What-wh-what?" She was trying to say something, but she was still stunned by the behavior she witnessed. "Why on earth? Where are your manners, children?" She turned to the group of kids who were laughing at me.

I still hid behind, with one eye on her, frozen,

petrified but started to feel the vibe that she was coming to my rescue; justice was going to be served.

"You know, children," She continued, talking as if she were Jo Frost, who was called Supernanny on TV for some reason, again she took a deep breath, "This is unacceptable. You kids will not be allowed to take part in the celebration, because there will be consequences for that kind of behavior."

As she said it, there was deafening silence filling that gap of loud noise from before, the kids froze; yet I was still stunned at their behavior in how they treated me, feeling that they soon would be paying a heavy price of $5,000 rent on the spot.

"Lewis," she said towards my direction, "You can come out and you can celebrate this luau." I slowly stepped out of my meerkat hole and walked towards a nearby table without making any eye-contact with the other kids. "He can be the only one celebrating because he was the one being laughed at by you kids." Our usually happy teacher's face was covered in deep frown lines, and I was surprised how the other kids weren't shedding tears. Still shaking, I was taking it all in what they had done that led to this point. I sat down on the chair to calm down and assess what had happened. I was to start the celebration on my own terms, but I turned to face the kids, too worn down to give the expected nananana facial expressions. I didn't get any gratification as they looked at me sad that they would be missing the party which only I was now supposed to enjoy. Like in *A Christmas Story* when the teacher found poor Flick after he stuck his tongue to a frozen pole after that triple dog dare.

When my mom picked me up that day the teacher talked to her. I didn't hear everything, only the words, "stand up for himself" and the big word "self-advocate" stood out. I heard my mom say, "He is trying, but still too young for that."

It was a mild yet tremendous blow to my isolation and yet it sort of built my confidence. This is a story, which shaped me into who I'm as a person. Shy, quiet, reserved on the outside, a warrior on the inside who doesn't want to emerge out so quickly but peeks out so slowly yet silently. Long ago, I knew I had it in me, that spark lit so dimly but the temperature was up to the Fahrenheit level where paper burns.

It's somewhat true that society thinks or assumes that we who are autistic are blissfully unaware of our own selves. But the opposite is true.

I can now totally see another perspective from viewing one's childhood from a photo album in a fantasy I lived then rather than seeing them in what it was and now that I know about my autism. Admiring, fantasizing over the photos, wanting to relive the moments some more as a ghostly apparition of present self-watching from afar. In the pictures I looked smiley, and I was keenly unaware of the world surrounding me. *Is my smile real happiness that made my childhood a great childhood? Is it my present satisfied self, seeing my own self as a kid differently? Or could I just enjoy seeing and hearing stories of what I've become?* Of course, they were all in the moment, not really to be posted and shared, but just for a dusty photo album, until my present-self got to see them and in awe of the picture as a digital references. Autistic or non-autistic, looking back to when I was little isn't a sign of Peter Pan syndrome, but it's seeing and reimagining how I was long ago, before my mom told me much later what I was. To also regain a sliver of that happiness for my present self like a mist of a manly cologne whiffing in my direction.

  A good childhood is seeing yourself in a single photo and quickly admiring how far you've come and that is a part of you.

  This Luau event is one of the vivid incidents I recall that started me questioning myself. What I mean by that is, I had this little voice within me asking me *why do I feel very different from the other kids?* And *what's making me feel like this?* and *why did this entire group of kids laugh at me?* Those questions sizzled at my own confidence and well-being. I wanted to learn fully about the truth of my own being within, what I could and couldn't do, how I was limited or was I unlimited?

*How did I get to that point? What led up to me knowing my intellectual disabilities?*

Little me sitting on a swing alone or on a field or just by the rows of thick pine trees, I would sit and fantasize a lot and often and be living in my own world: Pretending to be a singer at a live concert or a Jedi fighting the Sith and the Galactic Empire, while other kids rode in groups, I rode solo in the Millennium Falcon in hyper-space. All I had was my creativity and vivid imagination. I was just naturally put in a corner because of how alienated I felt, somehow other kids and I myself would put me in the corners of every room and every playground.

I was also a chubby kid at the time, plus my speech delay, so the chances of me being teased or worse, bullied were stacked high. Kids are the future, yet it does matter how they are raised whether they can be cruel or not. For instance, kids pretend-play and have such broad, bright imaginations but they can also do something mean to other kids if they are not the same size as a *normal*, average-sized child. Any fat shown on a child that seems abnormal to the average kid can only lead to any ruffians that walk by to act out and my world came crashing down.

I was often teased and one day in a game of tag, it was me who was "it," again. In my innocence, I pulled my shirt up to my rib cage and chased the other kids as they ran in opposite directions. At first, it started off as a fun, unique version of a game of tag, but not only was I chubby but I also could not run very fast. The kids loved it, and it was an inside joke that they continued to tell me that I was the one who was "it." It was a never-ending time loop almost like the game of dodgeballs, that one child is picked last and has to face a sea of flying dodgeballs, body-swerving like a car about to hit something on the highway. It was the constant feeling of being one excluded member of a group.

    They quickly learned how to take advantage of all the things wrong with me, in which there were three things: me being chubby, slow, and clearly isolated from the other kids. I experienced many who met the pure definition of what it means to be a bully; to exploit, make the most of another person's low self-esteem based on the differences on the outside and even inside of a person's body.

    During recess one day, I remember as if it's burnt into my brain, the other kids were playing some kind of cop-and-bad-guy chase where the kids pretended to be the police and only one other person had to be the bad guy running away, avoid being caught. Like that unique game of tag, they always placed me as the bad guy, always the one to be chased but not the other kids, when they always mastered to catch me. On the playground there was a ladder, the shape and size of an actual prison cell, boxed in, only open on the top, a square from top to bottom. Being chased, I made the mistake of climbing down into it and to their delight it was just the way they wanted to capture me, like they watched a lot of cop shows or movies; two held my waist like there were handcuffs scraped onto me.

    At first, I went along with it, struggling in a playful way. But the moment and the way they put me into that prison-cell-like ladder, it was like the scene of the 1973 film "The Wicker Man" but without the fire. The way they clamored blocked any gaps for me to break free, and while at first it started off a fun, thrill ride, my brain switched to survival mode and each time I tried to break out, the kids pushed me back inside. The screaming "don't let him out," became louder and louder in my own head. To them, it was as if they were shouting in their outside voices, but to me it was like being in a canyon where the voices echoed, bouncing back to me.

    I yelled, shouted out to a nearby teacher to extinguish the raging flames but he didn't look up or ignored it as *just kids play*" but it felt like a panic attack rushing out of the surface of my small body. I even tried to climb up from inside the ladder, but one boy had climbed from the outside and barricaded my way out, leaving me hopeless and stricken with panic. At this very moment, terror was rising out of me and I hoped for a teacher to be curious why all these kids were huddling around this one ladder, luring him or her to us. But no teachers were in sight to extinguish this whole situation, out of sight, out of mind. Where had all the teachers gone? At this point, I wanted to cry, felt hopelessly helpless and the kids certainly didn't have a tender side to poke at, no matter how I tried to break free, they just pushed me back in. It was like an intense game of Jujitsu where every time I tried to get a step ahead, they shoved me back. I would've done something to that point, but I didn't know what. I saw no options, nothing really occurred to my mind. The tears I had tried to hold back, now poured out.

    A glorious moment happened then: My aunt Ingrid saw the crowd of kids surrounding the perimeter of the prison-like ladder. She stepped closer and was stunned by what she saw. I inside of that ladder, frightened and bawling. She quickly stepped closer, pushed away other kids to get to me by saying "This is unacceptable!" and when she reached for my hand and helped me get out from the ladder, I was like a wet chihuahua, cheeks soaked, quivering. But the warmth and close range and protection of my aunt was comforting, and the kids knew; they had sad, *what-have-I-done* looks on their faces. I looked down and I didn't turn back; I just walked away with my aunt's protective arm tight around my shoulders. The kids hurt my feelings, they exploited me, so I didn't want them to get the satisfaction to see my tears after what just happened to me. Not in a million years.

You don't need to be autistic to be bullied, to be different. There are other factors for bullies to cherry-pick, to find the weakest, most vulnerable spot to just get a reaction for which they solely crave for. *And how does a kid start it, and all the others join in and support them?*

There is a reason why people who were bullied or even teased don't express that they were bullied. Because the memory of it is too painful to bear or to share. We wouldn't and shouldn't shame nor blame ourselves. And we shouldn't give the bullies the benefit of the doubt half of the time excusing them by saying to ourselves that maybe they were bullied or have a pretty bad upbringing. As if that would justify their behavior towards us allowing them to inflict pain greatly and internally.

My aunt and I never told my grandma nor my mom of the ladder incident. My grandma only found out about it after she read my manuscript. She asked me and my aunt both, why we never told,, and we both said we didn't want her to have to worry about one more thing. My grandma thinks that elementary school kids should be educated what it means for someone to be "autistic," so kids could understand from early on to treat us kids on the spectrum with silk gloves. But my grandma can be an idealist. Others will say "kids will be kids."

# CHAPTER 03 – QUESTIONING "WHO AM I?"

I also have good memories in elementary school. I distinctively remember the close friendships I had when I was there. I look back and exhale with a kind of reassurance and peace of what I once had but life took its way after I graduated from elementary school. Both the feelings of reassurance, peace and a sliver of regret, because after passing all the six grades – the last one after a second try - I could've exchanged phone numbers to keep and stay in touch, but we never did. Those are the friendships that I tried to recapture in my adolescence and adulthood.

After the elementary school graduation ceremony, I distinctly remember when one of my friends named Vincent walked towards me and started crying, realizing that it was the end of the era of elementary school and onward to great, big middle school. I remember bear-hugging Vincent, because he was the one friend who stuck out from the rest. He was also on the spectrum and his and my brain work similarly, and he has a slightly younger brother named Craig who is nonverbal, a sweet kid as much as Vincent. The friendship I had with them was like a comet that swings by Earth every 75 years, that's how rare and special this friendship was. The type where I want to reunite with them in adulthood at a local coffee shop and play a good ole game of catch-up. But it feels like this friendship was a long-distant dream so long ago that it doesn't feel it was possible.

A stretch from reality, in my own illusion, it is as if I'm estranged in some source, reaching out for the star in another galaxy to make it mine. Like, as if I'm Jay Gatsby standing at the end of the dock, looking from a distance, seeing nothing but a green light in cold separation, inevitably, reaching for something that was somewhat but not really there. Keeping that as a requiem, a token, a remembrance to what I once had, storing it into the dusty filing cabinet in my brain with all the other cherished memories. Not be like Gatsby who tried to repeat his past to get the girl, but to be a librarian of your own memories stored away in bookshelves and catalogs to look back for future lessons with the past lessons intertwined.

I had another friend in middle school. That friend was named Gabriel who happened to be my best chum, at least so I thought. We used to hang out at the movies or go to a restaurant or even go on a small trip to an amusement park with my mom, grandma and aunt. But as I write this, being held hostage by a pandemic, I've been wondering about that whole kindred spark of a friendship Gabriel and I had, and I've been asking myself 'was it a real friendship or a friendship with motives?' wondering if it was heartfelt and meaningful or insincere and meaningless. I'm walking around the block, thinking and rethinking my whole friendship with this person, as if I was in that movie, Wonder, about a boy named Auggie who was born with a rare medical facial deformity. There was a scene where another boy who doesn't have the same conditions as Auggie was told to be friends with him due to his circumstances.

    I was in the Special Education classes at the time but also intertwined with the kids who don't have any intellectual hindrances, so I bet Gabriel's parents or teachers told him he needed to be friends with someone like me so he could feel seen. I realize this now in my adulthood, realizing how much motivation he gained from being "that kid who befriends neurodiverse kids." It wasn't heartfelt, not his instinct nor from his heart. A friendship should be like planting a seed, patting it down into the soil and letting it grow and flourish and nurture along the way, not to rip out a plant from its roots and planting in your own garden for your own benefit.

    For Gabriel's case, who was neurotypical, the idea of being friends with someone in the Special Education classes such as myself was to show that he is inclusive. At first, he looked down at all the special-ed kids, thinking those kids don't think the same way as he, almost like he thought he would have to be a caregiver to those types of kids - us. But after he became friends with me, he realized, he might have thought wrong. He thought I wouldn't be able to grasp social cues and not be able to talk beyond my own territory of topics. I let him in like it was my house, inviting him to have coffee and chat and hang out with a cartoon to watch or for background sound. Also, I do remember that Gabriel was the sweetest boy ever, but too sweet. Any moderate curse words like, 'what the heck' or 'shoot' felt to him as if saying the F-word. As if Gabriel was the Governor of any state and he could outlaw or censor cursing, which would be the teacup calling the kettle black in his acceptance speech for the role of governor.

    You can't really outlaw curse words because that is how people express their emotions, in all different ranges. He was so offended one time when I said, 'what the heck' and implied he was so insulted, and said, 'don't say that, that's a bad word!' I looked at him and just thought 'huh?' and 'whatever' because he is a nice, sweet person, living in a South Park episode.

    That was all fine and dandy, until one day in the middle school stall I heard him talking to someone else using the "R"[1] word. *Why would he who says 'what the heck' is cussing, allow someone to use this word?* Whenever I hear it, I cringe - I

---

[1] The "R" word stands for "retard." From the Oxford Dictionary "a person who has an intellectual disability (often used as a general term of abuse)."

think it should never be uttered again. It's like in Harry Potter when someone was a pure-blood born with magical parents and called someone else a "Muggle." Gabriel never corrected him, never said "don't say that, that's a bad word." I waited until he and the other guy stepped out to leave the stall and was almost late for class.

    I do believe friendship should be and feel genuine and not be forced. Autistic or non-autistic, it should be and feel poignant and noteworthy unique and honest.

# CHAPTER 04 - SPECIAL EDUCATION AND ITS SHACKLES

"To Achieve, Or Not to Achieve"

*"It's not the critic who counts; not the man who points out how the strong man stumbles, or where the doer of deeds could have done them better. The credit belongs to the man who is actually in the arena, whose face is marred by dust and sweat and blood; who strives valiantly; who errs, who comes short again and again, because there is no effort without error and shortcoming; but who does actually strive to do the deeds; who knows great enthusiasms, the great devotions; who spends himself in a worthy cause; who at the best knows in the end the triumph of high achievement, and who at the worst, if he fails, at least fails while daring greatly, so that his place shall never be with those cold and timid souls who neither know victory nor defeat."* ~ Theodore Roosevelt

Hearing Gabriel's friend use the "R" word without being called out, was the straw that broke the proverbial camel's back. *What the heck" is bad, but the "R" word isn't? Or is it just easier to correct a special ed kid than a neurotypical one?*
It was my last year of middle school, and I had an awakening revelation: I wanted to break free

from being in the Special Education program, believing I had more to offer. I wanted to challenge myself, test into regular classes with non-autistic students no longer with students that were non-verbal or couldn't feed themselves or hold up a pen. That revelation did start full force, and I wanted to prove to others that while I'm now in the Special Education classes I could do more. Students with any kind of intellectual disabilities are treated differently than the students who don't have a source of learning disabilities at all. I was tired of being treated differently. So, I stepped into my own shoes onto the school campus, being that little engine that could, putting one foot in front of the other. I had to work harder than the other intellectually advantaged students to prove and to master what I wanted to achieve.

## CHAPTER 05 - MORE AWKWARD THAN A FIRST INSTAGRAM PIC

When I first hit thirteen, I immediately thought that I would want to dress in all black, long hair down my face, almost covering it and listening to nothing but angsty music that would reflect what I was going through. But there were no songs about autism, no hits about it.

My mom got married to my new dad just at the cusp of my teenage years. During their wedding ceremony, he announced not only would he take care of her, but also of me and not an eye in the room was left dry.

Early on, my obsession with black clothing and goth though caught his eye and he became very concerned. At one point he even read my diary, he said for my protection, which I've forgiven him for by now, but at the time I was not a happy camper. He had the misconception of the idea of adolescence, thinking I was super dramatic, but I had picked up storylines from my favorite shows and movies that seemed suitable to what I truly felt and wrote them into my diary. He thought those were my words and he and I butted heads at the beginning. Thank goodness he was very patient with me and I with him. At the time, I was just trying to fit into a specific group, the goth. With my autism, which is the opposite of the 'best of both worlds,' it was a 'worst of both worlds,' it's quite harder because the amplified hormones spin so crazily.

Sometimes you wonder about a person who is on the spectrum. *How do things come together for them and make sense?*

The end of summer that I turned fourteen, the age where my body and mind started to transform from a child to an adult, physically and mentally, I felt even more different, and I didn't know what it was. It wasn't the pungent odor from my armpits, or the red, disgusting bumps with whites on top growing like mushrooms onto my face as if I were a zombie in *The Last of Us* game. It was something mental, inside of myself, that I couldn't really explain at that time. But with each day I became more and more aware of it. Something was different about me.

I was living in the townhouse with my mom, my younger brother, my new baby sister and my dad. My younger brother was now four and he had started playing the Mario Bros game. I was sitting in the living room watching him play and I had this strange feeling, a feeling where the same sound was knocking at my skull repeatedly. In the game he was playing, Mario was walking and with each step he made a sound, a tapping, tap-tap-tap-tap-tap-tap-tap, which went on what felt like forever. The first few minutes didn't bother me, but then the tapping sound from the game grew louder, it pounded, almost repeating the sound at a much faster rate. And it all was caving in on me, until I nonchalantly, casually tried to joke about how I was hearing that same tapping over and over again, but nothing funny came out, until I pressed my hands against my ears. I couldn't take it any longer.

I gritted my teeth. My mom took one look at me and said she wanted to talk to me. I was relieved because now in the kitchen with her the sound coming from the other room was dampened.

"You should know, we have a diagnosis."

"A diagnosis?"

"The doctors think they know what you have."

I just stared at her.

Finally! After all the doctor visits she had taken me to, they knew what I had. Before I could even worry or ask more she said, "You have autism."

Just like that, my mom told me what I was feeling, and that it was known as *high-functioning autism*. I let it all sink in and for a second the word *high-functioning* made me feel smarter and at the same time off. That explained why for one I couldn't take this annoying repetitive sound any longer.

My mom added, "but don't let that define you, just consider yourself unique."

This makes me think, I feel like I'm one of you but different from you. At one time, the whole concept of autism felt like a singular line, but now it is a spectrum from the *high-functioning* to the *low-functioning*, a whole new universe of different people within.

    You would think that this revelation would shake me like an earthquake so large that the Richter scale would just break and shatter. Nope, it had not done this to me. But it did reshape me, and it explained so clearly many things from my youth why and what I felt back then but didn't know enough to analyze. I connect the dots from my youth, fully understanding myself because in some ways it was all good to learn that I have something that is not wrong with me but beautifully cracked that doesn't need to be nor can be fixed. It's something I will have to live with.

    "You will navigate through it," my grandma said.

    "We are right here by your side, all along," my aunt said.

    I also got a lot of encouragement from my mom and dad.

    The revelation was a beautiful poetic justice moment for me, and it felt like I was in a tall grass meadow, a sea of grass up to my thighs and a sunset ahead of me and me staring down at it like I'm Taylor Swift. But I was an anti-hero for a short, brief second. I didn't really want to look at the mirror, seeing a 14-years-old reflection of a boy with red-pink pimples and oily skin, wearing nothing but striped or solid-colored collar shirts or shirts with odd designs with bright colored pants that looked like jeans but not really jeans with now adding autism to the equation. Looking back at me, standing still and straight, I had to tell myself that I really am unique from the rest of other people and that indeed I should replace the word *autism* with '*unique* to stop myself from being insecure from having a label assigned to me and being a newly founded autistic individual.

This news added to the already angsty feeling of being a teenager. (Quoting Taylor Swift once again from her song "22"). Angsty, angry, happy, confused, complex in the best and the worst ways, all those feelings in the course of an hour.

It's to my own benefit and inevitable to find out who I truly am in order to fully understand myself; how to live in a world where they are not truly aware of autism and where some misconstrue the idea of it as a doom-and-gloom situation and just a total drainage and a burden to society – and often simply use the "R" word like those little old ladies from social services who did the very first assessment of me. Yes, I overhead my grandma tell the story, that when I was a toddler they came to her house where my mom and I still lived, to do an evaluation. After testing me and checking me out thoroughly they came to the conclusion that I simply would always be an "R." Yep, that's the harsh word they used and my family was so appalled it gave my mom and grandma sleepless nights. Later my grandma said that she thought it was because they were from a different generation where that word was still commonly used. For example, a friend of my grandma's got a college degree (BS) in 1975 in "Special Ed with a concentration in mental retardation."

I can truly sympathize with the people on the same spectrum, the same universe, who are as misunderstood as I'm that way. Today people don't use that word any longer (or at least rarely), but the stares I get or the way I'm being ignored sometimes can have a similar effect.

  A lot has been done, but not enough, to fully demystify the whole concept of autism or neurodiversity. Some people use social media as a sense of community and self-teach and learn more about the idea of autism as a diversity versus like most do: treating it like it is a special, rare case as if we're all at the beginning of the pandemic and we are infected with COVID; isolated and alone and everyone looks at us with pity.

***

  After summer and branded by my new label it was time for me to go to high school.

That first day was like walking through the brightly lit *Boulevard of Broken Dreams*, the name of a Green Day song. It was a new phase; a new chapter of my life was to begin.

I was now a full-on teenager and the real challenges began. I still had not removed those Special Education shackles and now I was supposed to continue the classes in High School. I felt unprepared yet tried to be ready for that new chapter waiting for me; and had to flip to a new page.

On the very first day of High School, ninth grade, watching a series of movies and television shows about high school could not have helped me prepare for what was to come. To cut to the chase, I hid in one of the 1980s-era, stuck-in-a-time-warp bathroom stall. I was sitting there on the closed-lid toilet, shaking, teeth clattering, inside those square wooden walls, which were riddled with misunderstood slang both marked and scratched on by high school students who came before me. Fabricating the worst in my mind, I was shaking. *What will happen to me next?* There was a stairway I had to climb to get to my classes where an upper-class student was harassing the freshmen. I didn't know how to get up there unscathed, so I preferred the safety of that stall. This is not what I had seen in the media. It was almost like I had forgotten to read the fine print, as if I read the entire, whole contract but missed the fact that the seniors would want to do that to us.

I certainly felt like a fish out of water, a fish in a toilet, waiting to get flushed down. I still felt so isolated because of my own intelligence or differences. I felt like Nemo who was in a plastic bag, pushing his way to the window and to the sea nearby.

The bell rang and I slowly collected myself and got up and left the stall. Step by step I braced myself sometimes forgetting to breathe as I walked to the stairway. Classes had started and luckily for me not a single senior was in sight. I had imagined the worst, but being late to class saved me; however, my special ed teacher didn't understand.

"You are late," the teacher said, with a frown on his forehead.

Definitely not the way I wanted to start out my first day there. "Sorry," I mumbled, not sure he heard me, but was just relieved that I made it to the class room.

"If you're late again your parents will be notified. This is your first day, so this is your grace period."

"Hmh," I nodded and sat down on the nearest empty chair. I really didn't like all that attention, I just wanted to hide. I couldn't tell him I was afraid of the upper-classmen; the entire class would have laughed at me. Not again!

That was my first day of high school. I knew

I needed to do better. I wanted to get out of the special ed classes even more than I was afraid of the seniors. I would prove to my teachers I didn't belong there.

    I just keep pushing, just keep pushing, just keep pushing, pushing.

## CHAPTER 06 - I CAN GO THE DISTANCE

"I'll be there someday, I can go the distance / I will find my way if I can be strong / I know every mile would be worth my while / When I go the distance, I'll be right where I belong." ~ from Disney's 1997 movie *Hercules*

I've experienced that people often assume that people with autism can't do just anything – *how could they have goals or dreams they want to achieve?* Or people assume that we autistics are coddled, or heavily dependent on another person for specific guidance and actions.

Yes, some autistic people need more attention like the ones who are on the end of the Autism spectrum. For example, the people who are absolutely non-verbal. Not that they ought to be treated like a lamb wrapped in 100-percent wool. They can't control that they might not be able to roam around the earth, independently. For instance, they shouldn't be put on a boat and pushed onto a lake, by themselves for them to figure the heck out on their own how to get back.

Some might assume that people on the spectrum use it as an excuse to just not have to deal with or face the real world and accept the hardships, the bitterness, and the toughness that reality is, or perhaps even view the world in rose-colored glasses.

But that is also wrong. I feel the difference about students who don't have any form of learning disability versus students like me who do have them. There is a distant shift between the two, as if the two parties (neurodiverse and neurotypical) lived in a parallel universe.

In the first weeks of my freshman year of high school, there was this uncontrollable notion, an awakening that continued to burn within me; more than ever I needed to prove to my Special Ed teachers that I was more than capable, had more to offer, and they needed to give me broader challenges. I felt like an outsider. I did not belong in that kind of slower learning environment. I was a fish out of water in the land of hermit crabs, begging to be thrown back to sea to fulfill this notion that I could do better. I wasn't sure whether or how I would fit into the sea, but I wanted to give it a try. I had to prove to them why I felt that way.

*So, what did I do to punch this four-walled glass box?* I had to work harder than the others, not to be a show-off but to produce evidence of my own driven passion, to demystify myself from the label of Special ED student and to show what it takes to be a high-functioning autistic individual. I didn't like the term *autism* or *autistic* at the time of my earlier days of high school it made me feel alienated and even made me feel more alone; made me feel that, *'oh, you have autism, you can't do x, y, z. As if I wasn't willing to try!* My brain rang 'BS' and I tried my hardest, anyway. I felt that in fulfilling that need, that will, that it had to turn my drive into achieving it.

Little was really done at my school from a point-of-view of someone who was in the Special Ed classes, who felt that they didn't belong there and who believes that they could handle a more challenging learning environment. There was no path out of it. It was my fire, my spark set ablaze, my heat vision shooting out of my eyes, which kept paving my own path. Yes, there were some teachers that didn't believe that I had what it takes. They thought that my ambitions were too big to pull off, that I was aiming too high and that I alternatively should aim lower like the rest.

"You are doing just fine here," one of the special ed teacher's said to me, when I approached him about the change. But I did have big dreams, for instance, I wanted to be a writer. I kept writing outlines of ideas of stories but always barely made it to the third chapter before another idea made me want to start another book, but I never completed one. I put writing aside for a while and decided to pursue photography instead. Boy, I loved photography (I still do) but back then, I generally just took nature pictures with my phone and called it photography.

There are things that I can do versus what I can't do, but many teachers often had me pegged, thinking they knew my limitations from the moments they heard "autistic."

Never blame a boy for trying, as long as I'm trying, but with regular support I could get even further.

I'll be there someday as long as I can go the distance.

## CHAPTER 07 – PICKING UP THE PIECES

*"If they give you ruled paper, write the other way."* ~ Juan Ramón Jiménez

    I reminded myself of the narrative still logged into my brain my family told me over and over: that I can do anything I put my mind to. But there are others on the outside who make assumptions that I cannot. Two narratives from the outside to the inside colored me more insecure, but a sliver of hope, confidence, and my warrior spirit were like 'no, no' and then lit up like small, little beacons that guided me away from those negative feelings. It lit up a pathway for me to travel down the dark tunnel that used to be an outdoor boulevard, now paved with dirt, and lead into a dark tunnel, but small lights guided me a way out, walking through broken, shattered dreams of adolescence.
    Being in Special Education classes was like being trapped in a glass box. A glass box with several layers of glass, making it more difficult to punch through to break free, like ankle shackles preventing someone from running.
    I had bigger aspirations.
*What do these dreams and goals mean to teenagers like me then?* We can dream but adults, especially teachers grab special ed students' little dreams and shatter them to little pieces, telling them

they can't or they receive excuses that they are too ambitious, aiming too high to reach, or that goals or dreams are too abstract, and that dreams could never be made into reality. On many occasions, I heard teachers tell that to the students who happen to be autistic and in Special Education classes. But I do feel bad for those other Special Ed students who have the disadvantages of being the way they are, because they can't read social cues at all; are in wheel chairs where you can see the physical challenge but the mental challenges are even bigger; they can't speak and some use a device to communicate which can be very slow and can take a lot of patience to operate and listen to; some use tubes to feed and the teachers would intentionally talk smack about them, as if the neurodiverse could not understand their surroundings. Some might not be able to, but since I was moved into a classroom into the same category with the ones on the lower spectrum with many more challenges than I, I could hear it all. I could feel with them, feel for them.

But some teachers didn't even try. "Why teach them if there are no results?" Or "I don't even think they understand me." *Did those teachers not realize we could hear them loud and clear?*

Some teachers in those classes even poked fun and said disparaging things about me, as if they were putting me to the test of what I'm capable of. Asking to be in regular classes, in their eyes. I was making an ass of myself breaching something that they thought was impossible, like a family of shoemakers wanting to be musicians. At the time, I would be angry, confused and just felt as if they would never understand my side of things, which blew my confidence to smithereens. *Was that their intention? To break me down, to break my spirits into continuously telling me how low my potential was?*

I always knew deep down I'm a rebel, according to what Juan Ramón Jiménez said about when someone gave me a ruled paper, I would take any pencil or pen I could find and write the other way. That brief quote resonated with me so deeply, because it is remarkably true. I do have the unlikely desire to think for myself and don't always have to follow the rules given to me. If only the rules don't apply to me, but people had already put me into a box, and it was hard to get out of it.

But, I know rules are rules and we do need them to balance the just and the unjust, but having too many don'ts and dos could only make young people wear a cool leather jacket, cool sunglasses, and walk through the high school halls like taking no sh*t from others isn't an option.

If they give you ruled papers, write the other way. If they put me in a glass box, form a fist the other way.

## CHAPTER 08 - FIRST EXPERIENCE: THE IDEA OF LOVE AND RELATIONSHIP

"Doubt thou the stars are fire, Doubt that the sun doth move. Doubt truth to be a liar, but never doubt I love."
~ William Shakespeare

I was still in the Special Education classes in the midst of fighting back for my own independence. And I read sappy, romantic Nicholas Sparks books and watched a soapy television series of the early two-thousands, *Dawson's Creek* and still watched the *Simpsons* and *South Park*.

There was a girl who sat a few desks in front of me. Her name was MacKenzie Conrad, and she had similar traits to mine. The first time I really noticed her was when she mentioned the show *South Park* and man, that show was my entire, very world. To an adult, it's funny but to a freshman in high school, it was funnier than funny. That kind of ignited a spark between her and me. I often quietly compared myself to the *South Park* character, Stan Marsh, because I had a growing crush on MacKenzie and felt extremely nervous around her like Stan, in the show, throwing up the moment his crush went near him. There were no cookies being tossed, but I was nervous, almost like I wanted to prove something like in any romantic novel ever written. I knew little or next to nothing about love, relationship and courtship at that age in early days of high school. The little I knew was from movies or shows. I was vicariously living through movies and shows, instead of experiencing life myself, like they're the textbooks to all my own problems and mysteries about life to come.

      As part of special ed, MacKenzie and I had to go to the job training, and it was mandatory to the max . We needed to learn what was expected of us at a job. Some days we would go out to the community; either to a restaurant or the back of a bakery at a local store called "Shoppers", and they would teach us new skills, like cleaning or baking cookies. MacKenzie and I were part of that group, and we were shuttled there by bus. We would sit next to each other talking about the latest South Park episodes. We often would laugh so hard tears would run down her rosy cheeks.

      It was incredible how close we were, having the same interests, for instance we both were very hard workers. When they told us in the restaurant to clean off the tables, she and I would race to see who could clean them faster and better, all while laughing and giggling together. She was also very assertive and when we saw that someone working in the bakery didn't wash their hands, she would say "don't be gross, wash your hands first." And again, we giggled. Laughter is the best medicine, and we sure did a lot of that.

    I would easily compare myself to Charlie Brown in the new 2015 *Peanuts Movie* where he has a mad crush on a girl that happens to have red hair. I had so much fun with MacKenzie, but I needed something more within me to prove myself to her somehow. Being with her so much, everything became blurry and fuzzy. I had this concept of a love relationship that I saw in the media versus what was real life. The media makes it all look so much easier.

    It was February 14th, Valentine's Day, and a few days before I had to think of something nice to give to MacKenzie. So, I asked my grandma to drive me and my friend Alexis to the mall to find that perfect something for MacKenzie. My grandma dropped us off with some cash. I wanted to buy something not too big, not too glamorous, but something from my own heart. A box of chocolates, a card or a small stuffed animal of some sort. I was thinking of a Rory-Gilmore-type gift-giving rather than an expensive Serena-van-der-Woodsen-type. That was not my taste and I also didn't have that kind of money. I also would scare her away by giving her large gifts as if I was the modern-day Jay Gatsby. Finding that perfect something at a Target, you know, something small like a chocolate box, but not something that would appear as if I was a rich person who would buy anything without knowing what they would like.

The idea of a cool yet a sweet necklace entered my train of thought. Seems like a sweet yet small gift for Valentine's Day, and Alexis agreed it was a good idea. So, I got the perfect necklace that matched MacKenzie's personality along with a cute, small stuffed animal. Giddy mixed with nervousness in the moment, I was excited to hand her the gift. It was Valentine's Day and of course, the spirits of Charlie Brown had taken over me entirely and my feelings were utterly ridiculous. I watched in the hallway as the "regular" kids, boys and girls exchanged red, pink and white gift boxes and roses, admiring their presents and imagining it was me. Alexis was to deliver the gift to MacKenzie herself due to my Charlie Brown-ness, too shy to do it myself. This sheer fantasy that I planted into the soils of my brain, waiting for it to spruce into a magnificent garden was that MacKenzie would love it and run up to me and hug me. I watched the spectacle of others enthusiastic hugging with envy and admiration and waited to hear back like staring into a blank, black soil after planting a seed, waiting to see a change in split seconds. It was a mixed feeling for me: the feeling of love in the air, worrisome, and living this false, surreal fantasy that this could be also me, as I looked on, watching other teenage students receive gifts of chocolate, flowers, stuffed animals, and photos of them posing all happy as I traveled the hallways. Hoping this speculation would form itself to reality for me too.

Like a chicken not having to man-up about my Valentine's Day gift to her, I waited it out the day after. But the excited revelation never came.

*\*\*\**

The day after Valentine's Day was a normal, regular high school day, until I entered the school campus. I saw my teacher standing there, staring at me with thin pressed lips and her arms crossed. She then rolled her index finger, indicating to *come here* to have a quick chat.

"Me?" I pointed at myself. She nodded. Being unsure as to why, I followed her as she walked inside the Special Ed classroom and there sat MacKenzie with her head down looking all solemn.

It knew I was in trouble somehow, but still wondered why. I slowly took a seat, it was a sheer, deathly silence, until a few moments later, the teacher cleared her throat to fill that deafening void of silence.

"So," the teacher begins, "Miss MacKenzie came to this classroom very concerned and frightened. It appears that you gave her a gift. A Valentine's Day present, perhaps?"

I looked at MacKenzie, folded arms, shaken, with a tense yet scared look on her face. *Was she really frightened? Of who? Not me!?*

"Yes," MacKenzie said so suddenly, "It was

a Valentine's Day gift. With a necklace, a chocolate box and a stuffed bear. My dad asked me about them and who bought them for me." Her voice sounded agitated yet like so innocent as if I were some creepy guy. She goes on, "It was nice and all, but it's a bit too much for my taste."

*Too much for my taste?* My heart started racing and the cheeks on my face felt hot.

The teacher clearly saw how MacKenzie was getting all worked up and simply patted her back, comforting, staring at me with daggers.

"Yes, that was a bit too much for her taste. What made you buy such a gift for MacKenzie?" Her voice as cold as ice.

I easily felt stunned by how condescending this whole situation was. I couldn't wrap my head around what I did wrong, everyone else had done the same.

"Um . . ." I started, shakily, who now knew my crush was an unintentional tattle-tail. "I - I . . . I didn't mean to make you upset. I was just . . . just trying to be nice."

At this point, this situation felt icy-hot, bits of it felt cold, with deathly silence and a mix of fiery, hot uncertainty. The teacher broke that silence once again, "I spoke to MacKenzie's dad and her to make clear that this will not happen again. Do you understand?"

Beneath the surface, I scoffed disdainfully,

but said, "This will not happen again."

"Apologize to her!"

*How did this all go so wrong? What could I have done differently?*

Reluctantly, I turned to MacKenzie, "MacKenzie, I'm sorry I didn't mean to make you feel uncomfortable."

She didn't look at me.

I got up and walked out the door, myself shaking, with a bad taste in my mouth. I walked out into the hallway with this uncertainty like I was Mrs. Maisel who had to uproot her ways of thinking about ideas, love, and relationships, after she left her husband and show.

That moment lives in my head rent-free to this very day; I really didn't mean to make MacKenzie uncomfortable. I was just simply being nice and again that whole bit was so, once again, confusing. The way MacKenzie acted all innocent, and the teacher acted like I was a creepy dude who needed to be taught a lesson. That day I learned so much about MacKenzie, my Red-Haired Girl, making me a bad guy. Walking out with these two, new seeds planted into the pit of my stomach: a grudge and a revelation. I walked to a nearby bathroom with shaky, trembling breaths, steadily to calm myself down. Hiding myself from the teenage society in the stall with ugly tears breaching out my eye-sockets, hiding behind the plastic-y ugly-tint green door, glazed with obscenity and a real, raw look of high school, much different than the one from some of the glorious Hollywood movies. I vowed to myself to never associate with MacKenzie again, for any other gift-giving from me to her in the near-future or anyone else for that matter and just remain distant acquaintances. On the bus trips to our work sites, we no longer sat together.

    Anything that happened that might've scared off MacKenzie showed her true colors; for me to even get into that kind of situation, instead of talking to me she chose to seek out protection from the teacher. I would make sure this would not happen again, of course she will never get a gift from me again. I did not want anything bad for her, would never, but wondered how she would function in the real world where a guy asks her out on a date, *would she just seek protection by hiding behind her dad or the teachers? Or was it just because it was me, the autistic one? Like fearing a bad date that would lead MacKenzie to hibernate like a bear in the dead of winter, hiding herself.*

    I thought the epitome of high school was having love relationships with someone. But, as I went through the first year of high school, it was nothing like that  the media often sugar-coats the whole idea of what high school should mean for teenagers seeing the facade and stepping into it – and they especially have it wrong when it comes to an autistic teenager.

I lived my own love crush experience, believing this sheer fantasy in the media would happen in reality without a director, a screenwriter and a production crew. It was a whole episode of *Dawson's Creek* smashed into a crossover episode of "insert creepy movie here" that tied to my own life. It was a sheer fantasy that was planted into my head, believing that could happen to me as if I was a character in those shows.

But, it doesn't and couldn't happen in the episode of the *Real-World* saga on Channel 3, because reality is different. There were no sappy, soapy screenwriters, a production crew and a director shouting *action*! and *cut*! and the only person who directed, wrote and produced, and starred in this episode of the *Real World* was me and her. There are no cameras, no scripts, just my own lens of my own eyes directing an episode itself, learning from it and improving on it.

I've learned the real concept of relationships as an autistic person, the hardest way at a very young age in high school which is inevitable, unavoidable, invincible yet there. This surely didn't happen to any of the neurotypical students. Love relationships aren't for everyone, especially not someone like me, not yet, but I did learn that high school was a time of my own personal growth and my own experiences, and it was best to not worry whether to be in love, thinking that I needed to grow up sooner, feeling then that I could be in my mid-twenties right about now.

I didn't tell any of my family members about what happened. I would have been mortified. *Would they also have judged me?* This entire situation was confusing to me. *What exactly did I do wrong?*

The bare necessity of an education is a building where students and teachers alike go to gain more information and knowledge about the past and bygone glory days and learn something from that past to lead the new generation of students to the future.

Not to just hang in the hallway, by the lockers either hugging romantically or giving a quick, or slow, small, little peck lip-to-lip. That is what I took away from this; not to have to worry about fitting into different cliques or crowds of other students who still clutch onto that shared sheer fantasy told by the media continuously and falsely. All those romance books and shows and movies about adolescence I've watched and read were lies, at least for an autistic young man.

*Lies or misinterpretation?*

By rushing time for romance to happen for me I got into trouble.

Or like watching HBO shows so early on that we could be confused about life and find in reality that things are dull, gray and boring?

That is the opposite of a bare necessity, and also like actively living in the digital world, without a shred of reality left to bear.

A few days after the whole Valentine's Day debacle, MacKenzie came up and talked to me. "Sorry about that, can we still be friends?" and after a few minutes she quietly said, "…. my dad gets that way."

The crush I had for MacKenzie completely disappeared. We still would say hi in-between classes, but not bring up what happened. You know, sweeping it under the rug while over time it collected dust, and now I briefly lifted that rug into the re-telling of this whole debacle: the story of my first crush.

## CHAPTER 09 - I WANT TO BREAK FREE

"To finally drive up to your house / But today I drove through the suburbs / Crying 'cause you weren't around." ~ Song "Driver's License" by Olivia Rodrigo

That phase of my life felt like a verse of that Queen song. *Yes, I wanted to break free* from being in Special Education classes due to my own ways of having more to offer than just wallowing in my own self-pity.

*Oh, you can't do it, it's gonna be too challenging for you.*
*There is nothing more you can possibly do.*
*It's out of your reach. Why aim so high?*
*I'm sorry, that can't happen so smoothly.*

Words like these expressed to me verbally affected me physically. The words really stung. The adults were saying I can't achieve something and that it would be out of my elements, out of my reach; patting me on the shoulder, as if any of my goals, dreams and aspirations were so high, higher than Mount Everest that I possibly couldn't reach them. The teachers just loved to make assumptions that I can't and couldn't do more due to my own intellectual ability. That was crap in my own sphere, in my own world, in my own mindsets. Teachers constantly telling me what I can and cannot do. .

Like any teenager, autistic or allistic, goes through different phases choosing the types of clothes they wear, what emotions they feel, trying to fit into the crowd that seems right, or just wanting to fit in, period.

    For me, it was sheer unhappiness when a teacher told me I cannot, and only made me feel like I was in a castle surrounded by a moat, and I felt so isolated like Rapunzel did in her castle tower along with the other Special Ed students. I got along with them perfectly fine. It was just that deep down into my inner core, my own gut feelings, I felt alienated, I was drifting apart from them. Not because of the way they were, I just felt so separate from the rest of the other students because of my own intelligence though I still engaged with them socially. Many of them didn't really have any neurotypical friends to talk to even though some can't be reached verbally and can't feed themselves, I know to some extent they feel bad or ashamed of the conditions they are born with, even if they can't express it. I sometimes felt that vibration of alienation coming from them, causing a blur, static line between the ones who are autistic and the ones who are allistic.

    Over time, it is soul-crushing and leads to burnout of having to adjust, to fit into an allistic world. It breaks my heart to see a person who can't talk, say a simple yet genuine 'hi.' Of course, if I were in the shoes and the skin and the mindsets of individuals who have so much trouble communicating, I would be frustrated, too, and maybe assume the worst in neurotypical individuals. I might be quick to belittle and berate the moment. I can actually talk and express myself pretty well, but like a bloodhound the neurotypical students sniffed out my autism immediately. Most of them ignored me and made me feel as if I was an adult talking in Charlie Brown making the 'Mwa-Mwa-Mwa' sound. Often, they didn't even bother to try to understand me as if I was made out of air. Since they didn't react to me, I can assume that to them I didn't exist.

Some don't say it out loud, but their facial expressions can be read from a thousand miles away and could feel heartbreakingly berating.

There is a quote from Harper Lee's *To Kill a Mockingbird* where Atticus explains to his youngest daughter Scout, how to walk in someone else's shoes in order to be fully immersed, emotionally and empathically. "You never really understand a person until you consider things from his point of view... until you climb in his skin and walk around in it." The neurotypical world could apply these wise yet simple words. It's an important life lesson for both autistic and allistic, neurodivergent and neurotypical alike to learn and understand each other, not to dismiss a neurodiverse person immediately. Try to master this every day for the future.

For instance, there is a call to *awareness* for

those who are autistic every April 2nd: Autism Awareness Day. That has me thinking. *How much awarenesses does the world need in order to finally get it?* How about acceptance? We should celebrate an acceptance day. I, now, would think that the world is already fully 'aware' with all the color blue and the puzzle pieces; but they are not good enough. What is good enough for an Autism Acceptance Month and Day is to let society fully immerse and embrace people, young, middle-aged, and old, who are diagnosed on the autism spectrum - misdiagnosed or diagnosed, doesn't matter. Therefore, society should further research and study more of the insides of the autism spectrums rather than the outsides. Focus on the cues, the hums, and the stimming of tapping, hands flopping, fidgeting, and spinning in response to their current, recent emotions, happy to sad to frustrated to overstimulated. Opening up their brains for those special nuggets that make those people three times more special, instead of abolishing autism as a whole without further researching more of it. I'm trying to find the great, amazing things about being an actual autistic person. Deep down, autism truly made the people on the spectrum unique and kind human beings. Far too kind. I sure do think just to spread awareness every time April hits is just stating the obvious that of course, we have to spread awareness. But to just use the Autism Awareness Month and

Day as a trend isn't awareness; to just snap a selfie with something blue and with a puzzle piece ribbon pinned to post on socials is not awareness.

A call-to-action is what's needed, not just awareness. Society's eyes are open wide, wide enough for autism awareness, but not enough for autism acceptance and required action. It's good for especially rural areas in America, where the concept might not be that well known, to receive autism awareness to let the people in the communities learn what it is and how it affects a person's life and tell it in the most positive light and with empathy. I'm sure some people are aware of it but throw in shades of stigma, self-pity, shame, and bitterness towards autism as if it's one of the worst, most horrible things a person could ever have and add feeling sorry for me and underestimating me as if my journey was much harder than it is in reality. I don't want pity from others. It's the worst feeling.

I sometimes throw a self-pity party, falling down this spiraling rabbit hole of self-doubts and underestimating myself even more than others do. Sometimes I'm agreeing with the nay-sayers. Like, making me a victim when self-pity is also causing me to be and feel less driven about the things I want to achieve. Like, 'poor me, poor me, boo-F*ing-hoo.'

Deep, knee-deep down, I know that autism isn't an illness that can be cured; it becomes an identity; my identity. I just have to know my self-worth and it doesn't happen overnight that I fully accept myself as an everyday, daily human being that is willing to accept his autism and try to not drive myself to pity.

It was almost like the word , *'autistic'* was soul-crushing, and my brain realized that there was something off, something was wrong. So, I had to rebrand my own intellectual ability in order to help myself from being more isolated than ever. I changed the word 'autistic' with allistic personalities, masked myself from it, shielded myself from that word, for the better. Almost like a defense mechanism I made to protect myself from any more damage. That went well with my own narratives of having more to offer, being more allistic, hiding away my autistic self for further safe keeping. I wanted to control most of the narratives, so I'm not written out of the *normal* group, so I did have to work harder than the other Special Ed students in order to achieve what I wanted. I needed to demand a learning environment I truly wanted and deserved.

## CHAPTER 10 - MOVE

My family was growing, and I now had a brother and sister. My parents decided that the townhouse we were living in was too small for us. We needed to find a bigger house for all of us. Houses in the area where we lived were expensive, so my parents wanted to move further South, where houses were still affordable.

The thought of having to start in a new high school gave me anxiety and sleepless nights. Yes, in my current school, kids were ignoring me and not taking me seriously but I also had some good times with the school having organized a buddy's club, where neurodiverse kids like me could hang out and we even had our own dances, which happened twice a year: annual buddy's club prom and buddy's club homecoming dances.

I heard all the horror stories about neurodiverse kids being bullied or worse being beaten up at other schools. None of that ever happened to me at my high school and I sure didn't want to find out what it would be like for me to be at another high school.

My parents and grandma agreed that I should finish up my H.S. diploma in my current high school, which meant I would now live with my grandma and only see my parents and siblings on the weekends, but they only lived a forty-five min drive away. I lived at my grandma's the first 7 years of my life and before my parents' move, I saw my grandma at least three times a week and spent a lot of time at her house already. Living there full-time if it meant I could finish the last two and a half years of high school in the school I was familiar with was not much of an adjustment.

Living there, I did more classwork than ever before, but homework was a big issue. Growing up in a single mom's household who was busy first going to school then working to make the house payments all the time, I didn't understand the seriousness of doing homework. I went through the motions of doing homework but never really worked hard. But, once I moved in with my grandma, she made sure I did my homework and together with her, my stubbornness and the determination in achieving goals that may have been beyond my reach and my sharpness of my 20/20 normal vision acuity and my peripheral visions became stronger and stronger.

"'Like it's hard?" Elle Wood from that Reese Witherspoon movie *Legally Blonde* would say and that was the same mindset I had: um, like it's hard. Yes, it was very hard. I didn't like being in the Special Ed classes, I didn't like how they babied me, lowering the expectations as if I could never stomach the bigger challenges. I sure did love a challenge and to set the bar a bit higher above my head, high enough to have to jump up with both feet. In Special

Ed classes, teachers would just set the bar so low it would be beneficial for all the students, non-verbals and verbals alike and the can'ts always rang true.

    I was a rare case, one that had and still has potential. A rare case who set and still is setting the bar higher. A rare case who is like a candle with a thin wick but still burning bright. A rare case like me being my own symphony, adjusting and harmonizing to my own tunes. A rare case of who is loved by all who push and raise the bars higher. A rare case was when I put a pencil to my temple, connected it to my brain and wrote on a ruled paper given to me the other way, a testament to my own independence with some self-determination.

~

    It was a constant battle. Teachers with best intentions for their Special Needs students thought they knew one hundred percent what was best for them and me. But somehow, they got it wrong in my case. I was treated as if I wasn't able to think for myself or couldn't walk, couldn't talk, or couldn't even have my own goals knowing what I wanted to achieve. It would be like Mount Everest to me, nearly insurmountable. I grew more annoyed being treated the same as the other Special Needs students on the other end of the spectrum like it would not be fair to them to let me seek out further challenges.

    It was not the feeling of thinking that I was better than them, but I felt that I needed more challenges to test myself. There were two students in that class I knew even from middle school that seemed chill, cool people. Their names were Everett and Dean, one was very hyperactive and had attention deficit hyperactivity disorder (ADHD) and the other had Down Syndrome. I respect them as friends and people who don't look like the *normal*, average people, but they still have hearts, they have feelings, they are not robots.

   The average, neurotypical person looks down at the people with Down Syndrome like there is something wrong with them. They are treated as if they were at fault, but they are not, they were born with it, demeaning those who were diagnosed with autism at birth, or two weeks or days after they were born. These kind of mean looks shouldn't be directed at people with Down Syndrome, or any unknown yet common, new factors that'll take a toll on their appearance and lives. Maybe a certain look and appearance on the face of an autistic person versus the face of an allistic, neurotypical individual often allows for guesses about what kinds of learning disability one could have. I'm sure people assume that the facial structures and expressions for someone with autism are a bit deformed and almost like a boy, or girl with cleft palates. The faces of a non-autistic, allistic person however are *normal* and often average-looking. For me, because I'm an autistic person but have the bold audacity in thinking for myself, people don't really *see* the autism, mistaken me to be a born, un-autistic person, like I was one of the *averages*, until I miss a typical, expected reaction. That is the reason why quote-unquote normal, that word lingers in my mind like it means something.

*normal*! 'NORMAL!

The word sits there in the center of my brain like it's when you ate the greasiest cheeseburger in the world, and it just sits there in your stomach.

NORMAL! 'NORMAL!

*normal normal*

It's like the scene in that 2004 Pixar movie, *The Incredibles* when Violet at the dinner table asks, "what is normal," trying to fit in while being an outcast who has powers. Superheroes trying to fit into an idyllic, suburban neighborhood with the non-superheroes, everyday folks with non-superpowers striving for day-to-day life.

NORMAL! NORMAL! *Normal.* NORM-AL?

The word just feels like a misplacement, the meaning of that word is like trying to be *normal*, filtering your true self to display a watered-down, plastic-y version of yourself. *normal* is like playing by the rules without you having to break nor bend them, but God forbid if you mis-react to an expected behavior. But I have to remember and tell myself that for regular activities, like getting your driver's license or permit, going to a local coffee shop or at the mall, people don't really care whether you act *normal*, as long as you stay out of their way. They do seem to care about the interactions, but not the passing-by, because they also have their own lives to deal with and don't throw others' lives into the mix. They just don't have time. So, I need to stop taking myself so seriously. This quote from the CBC shows *Schitt's Creek* is appropriate when Alexis Rose tells Lewis that 'people aren't thinking about you the way that you're thinking about you." To me, that is such a profound quote, and it is so true that people don't really care about you the way you do care about a certain part of yourself. They do but they don't.

People care more about themselves and don't really care about all aspects of you until an extreme line has been crossed. For instance, any kind of disturbance of someone talking to himself – like I sometimes do - or swaying side-to-side, oblivious to his world – like I, or to the extreme, someone shouting, yelling out vulgarities that could feel frightening of any kind, whatsoever (which I don't do). Other than that, people in the real world have their own safe place, their safe haven, their own versions of walking down a peaceful forest and don't pay attention to what's normal. Their peace is only shattered if they see "abnormal" behavior.

I do have potential to reach that "normal" expected state, because I don't want to be singled out. I'm autistic . . . so, what?

My inner warrior. My inner flames; which ignite sparks. Where does it come from? It's not a pleasure to burn, but it is a pleasure to ignite my own fire of not cockiness but self-righteousness.

I don't have special powers to control, to manipulate fire, for example, but I like the idea, the concept of it all. The concept of a metaphorical fire that has been set alight, been displayed and represented on a candlestick, glowing as a beacon out of a scary, dark tunnel.

Fire wasn't created to destroy, but to light up the blazing path that is burning bright and to lead to the end of a dark tunnel. Something that is inside me and inside my heart that is both glowing and raging, not meant to be a response to anger, but instead it's a response of I can do this; I'll show them all, prove them all wrong.

That was a gift given to me as a baby and as a small child and I got to utilize it, use it to work harder than ever before: My family saying, "You can do this!"

## CHAPTER 11 - I CAN DO IT; I'LL SHOW 'EM

There was a regular school meeting called the Individualized Education Plan (IEP) that my mom and I attended twice a year from the time I was in kindergarten all the way through high school. It was a meeting provided for the students and their parents or guardians to consent to a plan to help me improve academically and socially. Think of it as a check-up on how I'm doing in class overall and what goals new and old needed to be met and any concerns about me from the teachers or parents were brought to everyone's attention. My mom and I usually were the only ones in the room with five or more educators. I sat there while the adults talked about me and my mom just mostly nodded.

I was getting nowhere by asking to get out of special ed and had been in that position for a while now trying to prove to other Special Education teachers of my own bigger abilities within my intellectual disability. I wanted them to see he is able, not the label, because there are so many things that I'm capable of being and doing. For me it was clear; the Special Education teachers looked at me as if I were exactly like the other students in that class, but I had a fine print in the bottom of my own Terms and Conditions that said I can do more but they refused to read it, just assumed I was the same case. Maybe a few understood what I was going through, but deep down, they didn't want to bother.

I was kind of like Luna Lovegood, a *Harry Potter* character who was known as odd and strange and abnormal. At first on the surface of it all, they judge me by first impressions without first getting to know someone like me, assuming they already know.

I felt the special ed accommodations were good within my school, but outside of it all, leaving with a navy-blue, or black cap and gown, are those accommodations still useful when we leave high school? We made it so comfortable for neurodiverse people in school, *but why, what, and how would we continue that even after we neurodiverse leave the premises? What would a special ed education give us?* Those questions shall be answered not now, but in time, it will, but don't just ask, don't just talk the talk, go walk the walk.

Finally, at one of the first IEP meetings in high school, my mom made it clear to the IEP board that the goal this year should be to get me out of special ed classes that I should be allowed to try some of the regular classes. At first the educators looked at each other, then stuttered "but won't that be too hard?" and my mom said, "give him a chance." Finally, they agreed they should try, and my mom asked that the board define what was needed for me to just do that "try?" It wouldn't be easy, they said, and it would be a lot of work and I could fail, but still I couldn't believe it, they finally wrote the goals into the IEP to get me out of special ed and for the teachers to give me additional assignments so I could prove my case.

Although some of the Special Education teachers were very helpful and wanted me to achieve this goal and really aimed to make a difference in a student's life, there were others who thought otherwise.

Like Mrs. Project, she was the one teacher in those classes who talked behind my back and was super passive-aggressive towards me. One time I was across the hall from her, I heard my name, and my ears perked up. What was she saying about me? To make her case that I have no broader potential within me, and it was a complete utter hoax? At the moment, what was she trying to tell me? Saying that I was the same as the rest of the other special ed students, no better, and that this was just a phase. This was her way to gaslight me into thinking that I have no shred of potential. That made me feel so frustrated and I questioned whether I could be faking how I truly felt. Frustrated living with the stigma of being autistic in the educational system and above all, mostly frustrated about the sheer audacity in which Mrs. Project dared to question my goals. I was and am still a nice guy who always keeps my emotions in check, so I wouldn't go off on her, be rude or come off snippy. So, I did a cool, calm, collective approach where I just took in the negative, spiteful energy because she was the teacher, and I was the student, and it would not be a good idea to cause the classic teacher-student headbutt.

And often when I was in her classes, I felt like I was in a reverse Charlie Brown special where every time I said something, Mrs. Project like some of the students I tried to talk to would again only hear me through the sounds of a muted trombone. Why's that, you might ask? Like I've said before I was a fish out of water, I felt that I wanted more and did have the potential, but not everyone agreed.

But I worked harder than most of the other students to prove my point that I can reach that fullest potential I've wanted since stepping onto the brownstone of school.

I don't want to believe that my autism should hold me hostage, should really limit what I'm capable of. So, to repeat, I worked hard to prove to them that I belonged in the independent classes, but without realizing that it could be a little more challenging than I thought. We shall see.

My grandma got a tutor, Ms. Brown, who came to my mom's house every Saturday. Ms. Brown taught me how to count money and recognize the different coins and the different bills. I memorized all the famous faces on the money, I could recount each by heart easily and over and over again, but if Ms. Brown asked me to add the amounts together in numbers my brain just blocked. Math is incredibly hard for me, if not impossible. My grandma says that "somewhere my math brain synapses are just not connecting."

But my work ethic was through the roof, I did everything I was told thoroughly to the point where some of the Special Needs teachers were impressed in how I ran things so smoothly, like Michael Jackson had something to do with it. Okay, I will tone it down a bit, don't want to be too arrogant. I knew I did have that inside me, so driven that I put my autism aside in order to do what I'm told and not use it as a passport, as an excuse for what goals not to achieve.

After lots of studying with my aunt, and now visiting a math tutor weekly, then bringing up my grades in quite a few of my subjects, I had shown my true potential and finally oh finally was approved to move out of the Special Ed classes to General Education with the other allistic, neurotypical students, where I felt I truly belonged.

This moment came without much fanfare. "Yes, you can sign up for regular classes," was all I was finally told, and a note was pressed into my hand to take home to my mom and grandma. And another reminder of the special ed board members, that I needed to work on "advocating" for myself. "Your mom put in this request; it should have come from you."

Hmh, I had asked so many times to be moved

up from the special ed class, I just was never really heard. They insisted, the single most important skill I was still missing was advocating for myself. In their defense, my mom and grandma and aunt always reminded me to "stand up for myself," make my needs and wants known and to advocate for myself. Why that was so hard for me, I just don't know. In my head I'm always advocating for myself, I just need to vocalize it and turn it into action.

Still, this was one of my proudest moments of my high school career, because moving to regular classes I just knew would allow me to shine with all my glory and be a role model to these other autistic students.

I couldn't wait to sign up for one of the "regular" classes.

While my fire continued burning bright, ablaze by my own fiery path formed as beacon in a dark tunnel, I dug up my hobby from the rubble from my own soil.

I had (and still have) the absolute passion for photography. I enjoy the thrill of walking somewhere beautiful, anywhere in nature, and just love to capture what I see with my phone to be put up on socials. Forests, trees, sunsets, lakes, streams, fauna, anything. Videos, pictures, you name it. I'm certainly not here to gloat and you will see, what I'm here to tell you about that this isn't the case.

It was continuous battle of raising another

bar, when a few teachers again thought it was just a phase for me to love photography. They thought I just liked the aspect of taking pictures. They thought I was a punk who wanted a name for myself who had a pride the size of a horse pill to swallow. The teachers too often and even I still viewed me as the same kid from Special Education who just now transitioned to General Education. The label of autism was like a giant diamond ring that was so big and awkward, that it kept getting caught in something like my sweatshirts and my freedom. It was cumbersome. Not that I could control the fact that I was born and diagnosed with this stigma-slash-identifying label that regulated where and what I wanted to be. I wasn't truly ashamed of it, yet I was in constant battle with myself and my own identity, even though I truly did rename and rebrand it to another word: unique. But it still wasn't enough to satisfy my own autistic side, like a guilty conscience kept reminding me not to be someone I'm not. To beautify and to embrace my new freedom in regular classes in all its glory without shame or stigma, it all was growing too slow like a watermelon seed inside.

    Despite all the doubts from teachers and myself, I signed up to the high school photography class, in addition to the typical required English and math classes. Photography would be my very first regular class. I wanted to be in the class to learn new techniques. I just knew how my brain works, and I could see the world through a much broader yet beautiful lens of a camera that'll tickle any movie directors or big-time photographers' fancy.

And it was the kind of photography class where you snap a photo from an old camera, and you take the film from it to be illuminated in a dark room with an eerily red light overhead. It was the 20th century way of taking pictures.

The teacher Mrs. Moyer had lots of detailed instructions she handed out which were typed on paper and then let the students work independently. Mrs. Moyers wasn't at all into teaching the wonders of capturing pictures that you could see with your eyes and try to emulate onto the camera. She wanted us to follow some written down rules. "Read the instructions."

*Where was the deeper insight? Where was the magic of pictures?* That style of teaching wasn't working for me, not so fast.

Mrs. Moyer mentioned I missed a step multiple times. Ok, I went back and tried again, but her complaints kept coming to the point I was getting very nervous to even make a move. Sometimes she would get impatiently mad at me, like I was just an imbecile, a nut-job in thinking of myself as a photographer. She didn't have any interest, nor patience in enlightening me or any student more about it. This way of teaching – just being given instructions – oh, that was very strange and new to me and how could I have known that class would only teach students photography that way?

"Read the instructions and ready, set, go!"

Sounds to me, it's evolving but backwards and I didn't know back then phones in the future would get to that point where you could just take a gorgeous photo of a beautiful sunset or the castle at Magic Kingdom without a bulky Nikon camera. But those old cameras are not going to fade fully away anytime soon. It's just that the teacher didn't have the patience to teach me and every time I asked a question the response was *why-you-bother-nor-do-I-care*. The saddest of it all was that I had just come from Special Education classes and Mrs. Moyers wasn't trained to help me reach the higher bar, thinking I was just a helpless, little person. As if we were all Toph Beifong in "Avatar." No, a disability shouldn't be limiting, only because a dozen people just wanted to lay the ground rules to us saying that *we can't do it*. Like this narrative always danced in my head so often that I was worthless and didn't seem to matter, setting us all up for failure. Oh, boo-hoo, you don't have to feel sorry for me because it was the past and I'm not expecting closure, because this book is a real treat of a free therapy session because I'm only telling this because let's say someone at a local library or at a bookstore stumbles upon this book and glances at it and reads a few pages and feels heard and seen. Well, that is the intention of this book because I know I'm not alone, definitely in the moment where some teachers and that photography teacher didn't see me worthy to be a photographer – it wasn't all laughing-materials. And our minds often play tricks on us in thinking that we are worthless, and our voices don't matter, but don't really believe that for a second!

During the fourth week of the class, walking into the photography room, Mrs. Moyer, who usually looked at me with indifference, stared behind me with a huge frown.

"You left the door open!" She yelled. Her eyes were like daggers.

I turned around to check because I knew this much from the instructions that the door needed to be closed because the incoming light would destroy the photos we were developing. I carefully had tried to shut it behind me when I entered but Jason had walked in right behind me, and I held the door open for him; he must have left it open. I didn't pay any attention, after I had handed the door off to him, but how quickly the fingers were pointed at the former special ed kid, me, because of course. I waited for Jason to say something, but he turned his back and just sat down. From that moment on Mrs. Moyer was even more annoyed with me. She mumbled "They don't pay me enough for this." When I was sure I followed all the film developing steps everyone else did, take out the film and carefully place it on top of the acidic solution and watch the black-and-white film develop and more, she thought I was too slow and always found something to nitpick until one day she sent a letter home to my grandma: "He is not ready for this class…"

My grandma rolled her eyes at the letter. "How difficult can photography be?"

Very difficult for a neurodiverse person, according to Mrs. Moyer.

Beats me.

I was too slow, but I don't ask for special treatment because of my autism, I do, however, need a bit more time.

When I told the story of the open door to my grandma, she asked why I didn't mention Jason. But she knows I don't like to cause trouble. My grandma said that to stand up for oneself was not causing trouble but that it's called to self-advocate. That word seems to follow me throughout my entire life.

I absolutely still needed to learn to self-advocate.

Those disappointments and the F-ups were the oil sprayed on the flames of insecurity inside my inner core, to prevent me from reaching higher and to be on my own terms and the teachers wanted me to just chug along the tracks with little to no purpose. "Is he giving up yet?" "Can he see that he belongs back in Special Ed?"

After receiving that letter, my grandma

joined my mom in attending the IEP meetings. She wanted to hear first-hand what was going on. How could anyone flunk photography?

The first IEP meeting she attended was eye opening to her and me. The layout and the format of the teacher's presentation was to always speak to my mom about me in the third person, not first. I was sitting there, and they would always talk to my mom about my goals, as if I wasn't in the room.

My grandma sized up the meeting and just said, "Lewis is right here; can you please address him directly?"

This didn't really occur to me ever before in all the years of attending IEPs that they were doing that. That shred of conscience that was brought to my attention by my grandma who spoke to that so powerfully.

And I wasn't angered or outraged by that at all in the moment, but it was like a swirling cloud over me that it didn't even occur to me at all ever before and it surely didn't occur to my mom because that's how the meetings had been since elementary school. But now I was in high school. I was so used to all the adults discussing my future would talk about me, instead of with me. And now that cloud had been lifted away by my grandma, I could see clearly, nothing but blue skies and was fully aware of what was happening in those IEP meetings.

I could speak up for myself.

It was just another example of me not knowing how to self-advocate.

*Hmm? Self-advocacy? Now what does that mean?* Definition: speaking up for oneself and one's interests, and it is used as a name for civil rights movements and mutual aid networks for people with intellectual and developmental disabilities (according to *Google*).

*Yes, but what does that mean?*

Something that came to mind about that in a scene from the third *Harry Potter* movie where Ron was reading his tea leaf, reading the future, "you're gonna suffer, but you're gonna be happy about it." And that came to mind because it was and is still so true about myself where even though I know the definition for self-advocacy and others drill that word and definitions into my cerebellum it's just so hard for me to get it. Like how Aang, in *Avatar: The Last Airbender* couldn't learn the concept of earthbending, it is me with self-advocacy because 'if I try, I'll fail, but if I don't, I'll never gonna get it. I feel like I'm caught between a rock and a hard place'. But I do know that I'll eventually get it and understand it step by step because I'm also human, not some AI Intelligent machine, I'm going to make mistakes and not grasp anything and everything and that's OK and it's not worth beating myself up over. Yeah, try telling that to me in the moment when I don't understand it. But in hindsight and in the near-future I will know it and grasp it. Knowing me, I will slowly but surely grasp the concept of self-advocating for myself because I know that if I don't speak up firmly for myself and for my own needs, who else will? My grandma, mom, dad and aunt won't always be there for me. I have to learn to do this on my own.

These types of experiences like the photography teacher kicking me out of class and the adults talking about me and instead of with me, gave me more gasoline to keep me on my personal quest of expedition and self-discovery. Almost like cuing that *Mandalorian* theme song, muttering to myself "this is the way" as I swiftly walk into the yellow-orange desert of Tatooine.

(I know easier said than done.)

...But it's true, our brains tend to fixate on the negatives so naturally and normalize the negativity as a concept rather than just develop a coping skill to not feel sorry for ourselves. Yes, at the moment it may seem that way, but I promise you that over time I can shake the negatives, and you'll see a beautiful picture and laugh at it in hindsight.

I think it's important to balance out people who are flat-out awful and people who are nice and decent. But about the flat-out awful ones, the ones who put you down, the ones who think you can't accomplish anything or the ones who have zero patience with any type of delay. The ones who are blunt and brutally honest and see everything black and white, normal or not normal. In the moment, their commentary stings and yes, it's just not right, but in hindsight, later much later I can look at them as faded memories that don't expect closure.

Today, my today-years-old self (as the cool kids calls it) I still love photography, still love to learn and try new concepts and I know that there is no 'skipping to the good parts' in life and in-between is only work and working on yourself on the things you want to do and drown out the noise from those flat-out awfully brutally honest and blunt people. When I have a vision in mind, I just write it down or type it out, whatever it may be. That'll be my first step in doing it all and then I try to envision it by displaying it in my mind to ultimately have it in front of me. It could be just googling an inspiring Ted Talk on YouTube or if none of those ideas works, I'll entertain myself by creating and uploading videos to my Instagram or TikTok accounts.

I tell myself that I'm limitless and just try, just try, and it doesn't have to be a 100-percent perfect and as long as I try and keep trying, progress will be in order. Those are also the words my family keeps telling me and I try, and I try, and I try.

I made and continue to make my points about what it means to be an autistic person and not just use the label as a trendy trend that is trending on

Twitter. Like an onion, autism has more layers than what you can see. There's more to me than meets the eye, the tip of the iceberg, any other metaphors that have to do with… a problem that seems small yet is tremendous when taking a look at a bigger picture, not just the golden frame bordering it. When people kept telling me I couldn't do something, it was like brushing dust off my shoulder externally, and I wanted to tell them they were wrong, but internally it slowly made me feel insecure six feet under within me. Insecurity burrowed deep down within me, but I often filtered it like a Brita water filter to alter how I was truly feeling. Altered that icky, insecure feeling and cleaned it all out to make me the warrior with the I-can-do-it attitude.

# CHAPTER 12 - ENGLISH CLASS "JUST SHAKE OUT THE NEGATIVES"

### "You Can't Always Please Them All"

I got what I wanted (not in a way as a spoiled rich teenager gets his or her way). I was unhappy where I had been, but I had finally gotten out of Special Ed; out of the tap-water-filled aquarium and into a salt-water ocean that I dreamt of for so long. But I realized quickly that I have to work much harder than the neurotypical students in fitting in and continue swimming in the ocean where I belong, not to swallow water and gag, trying not to screw it up.

I was finishing up my sophomore year in high school, and my English teacher Mrs. Valery Cruz had me more stressed than any teacher up to that point. She made the photography teacher look easy. Mrs. Cruz was the strictest English teacher I've ever come across then and she set the bar high and was strict with not just me but also the other students; it was just her nature. She gave multiple homework assignments and specific, short deadlines; if you didn't turn them in on time all points would be deducted. At this time my grade was a full-blown "F." She clearly thought that I was just some punk, some incapable student who doesn't give a sh*t about the art of education and learning as if I was the baddie in some 1980s coming-of-age story.

The homework was piling up but there was no help given and I knew that parts of it was me not self-advocating, again! And it showed in this English class. I wanted it to be done, wanted to speak up but the only problem about the whole self-advocating thing is that … I don't know how to. I couldn't even tell my mom or grandma or aunt. Others make it sound as if it was super easy to do so, but it's easier said than done. *Why am I afraid to speak up for myself?* I know it has to be done to have my needs met because if no one ever does it at school, who else but me?

Maybe the reason why self-advocating is hard for me to understand is because I'm always very self-sufficient and like to try myself the first time before letting others help me, just to see how I can do it. I also know that I'm so very much inside my head that I have a hard time letting others in.

This English teacher, the strictest teacher I knew until then, really didn't have the patience to teach me how the English sentences are structured and often we read old poems from poets who lived at times where science and new things were witchcraft and bogus intertwined. She assigned very hard homework about the poems and reading passages that I was reading in class to see if I comprehended them, most of them were in old archaic English language, like the people back then spoke as if they were all in a Shakespeare play. And most of them I did not understand, and it again felt like Mrs. Cruz was laughing at me as if again I shouldn't be in her class, thinking that I was stupid. But a part of me wouldn't give in to despair and just give up, failing the class and I tried and tried and somehow it wasn't enough nor was she ever satisfied. Oftentimes she would call on me at random in class just to see me stammering and acting like 'look at this kid. He shouldn't be in my class if he doesn't know anything!' so I felt like a laughingstock, but luckily other students weren't laughing, I think they just felt bad to see me stammering and not understanding the passages while Mrs. Cruz just stood there and took it all in with arms crossed in front of her. I think some of the students felt bad that she picked on me and had the audacity to treat me that way without any help.

  Over time, the class felt harder and harder, like a video game bumped up from difficulty to extreme, without no guides to guide me through a walkway and it certainly felt hopeless, and I didn't know what to do.

  Finally, my grandma received an email from Mrs. Cruz saying she doesn't think I was ready for her English class. My grandma was surprised because I had not told her about the problems at all and she was disappointed that I didn't tell her sooner. She looked at my blackboard for the first time and gasped. "You have not done any of your homework in time."

Yes, that was because I had no idea how to do it, but of course I never told her. My grandma's solution was to get me a tutor and additionally, she and my aunt spent hours and hours, days and days practicing English grammar with me.

In the meantime, I had no choice but to drop out of that class to another much lower-level English class to slowly help me understand the structure of the English sentences and what made up a paragraph with the periods and semicolons and whatnots. It was clear I was not taught much during my special education classes, and I had a lot of catching up to do.

Mrs. Cruiz thought if I took her class, I should have the prerequisites and she didn't have any patience whatsoever for someone who didn't, and ultimately, I realized how much I had been missing being in special ed.

## CHAPTER 13 - CHOIR

My family encouraged me to try out for choir and while at first, I thought "I can't really sing," they kept pushing and I decided to try out.

The day I tried out for choir I walked into the spacious music class room and some of the kids were already seated. Mr. Brandt stood in front of the class; a man who wore a grey cardigan. He smiled at me as I walked in, and he smiled at everyone which immediately put me at ease.

He asked us to introduce ourselves and to say why we were there.

I just said, "I like to sing." He smiled again. There was no doubt in my mind that he didn't care I was autistic.

Soon after, we all got to practice musical notes, no questions asked. He never asked what experience I had in singing or anything about my background. He talked us through the structure of a song and then asked us to do a vocal exercise. Each of us had to sing a line from the song "Bridge over Troubled Water".

He demonstrated it for us, his voice perfection and smooth. It was my turn to sing a line, but I didn't really know that song, and hesitated, even though the words were displayed on the power point overhead.

Mr. Brandt asked patiently "You said you

like to sing?"

I nodded. "Mhm, yes."

"If you like to sing, then you can sing this line." He smiled again.

I just looked at him, I wanted to sing, but nothing came out, and he just patiently repeated the line for me.

I again froze and he said, "Why don't you just hum it?"

I slowly started humming and to my surprise my voice didn't sound bad at all.

"Now sing the words."

I read and sang the words from the PowerPoint.

*"When you're weary, feeling small, when tears are in your eyes, I will dry them all, all I'm on your side, oh, when times get rough."*

I stopped.

Mr. Brandt smiled. "You are our perfect baritone," he sounded excited. "We have been missing the lower range and you will fit right in."

These words stuck with me and still today are music to my ears, because that was the first time since elementary school that a teacher gave me a compliment. In a regular class!

I had been so very nervous, but I shouldn't have been, because from that day on, the very first day of tryout, the choir teacher Mr. Brandt accepted me and made me part of the choir.

Choir was a place where I felt more home than I had felt in any other class, and I felt more comfortable than ever before. Every time I walked into the large choir classroom, I felt comfortable and secure and I felt a higher level of glee when we did vocal -tests: *do-re-mi-fa-so*. Absolutely fantastic. And when we went to a church that was not too far from where our school was to perform and in our fancy-schmancy tuxes, that each of us had to purchase in order to be part of choir, ready to sing our hearts out as we looked so presentable, it made me feel more alive and part of them.

Part of them!

It was a brand-new feeling - something that I had never felt before. I felt completely included.

Choir also opened up a new double-door for me and that is a whole new world of Broadway musicals. The choir teacher was my most favorite teacher of all time and some days we watched movies like *West Side Story,* and we became kind of a mix of Broadway and movie critics judging how the performances were done in such majestic, magnificent ways.

This blossomed my interest in Broadway musicals, and I fell in love with the musical numbers and often loved to poke fun at how inaccurate musicals could be but still adored them anyway.

Choir was a place where I made friends and easily fit in without the usual effort to please them into liking me. I learned that these theater students were so easygoing and witty and quirky that I admired them so much that I wanted to become quirky and witty. It was very easy to be in sync with them and I grew more confident and comfortable around them. Every time we'd go out to perform at a local church or in the school auditorium in my form-fitted tux, letting out my baritone voice, I felt like I was in my element. But every time in the beginning of every concert performance, I always felt so, so, so, so nervous that butterflies shuddered my stomach. My grandma said, " It's OK to have butterflies just try to make them fly in formation and put that energy into your voice." And I did. At the end of every concert performance, I was feeling good like Nina Simone had something to do it with. Every time I was on any stage with my Choir group, in my tux and my voice completely harmonizing with the others made me forget that I have autism, made me feel so very much included. I often compare my time in the choir to the movie "Pitch Perfect". I love that movie; I watched it over and over because it reminded me of the good ole days of singing along, fitting in very well with the others.

    The two whole years of high school choir by far were the best experience of my school-life.

    Those junior and senior times of my high school days really improved my confidence, and molded me into a new person. Choir was my outlet to grow even more comfortable and confident. It's not just that I simply put my own autism aside, I had accepted myself for being an autistic human being, but often I felt and still feel so angry, frustrated at myself for being the way I am. The song "I want to break free," by Queen comes to mind. I know that it isn't my fault I was born the way I am and I should take more pride in that instead of dissing it, to make myself feel like I have to have something to fulfill.

   To fulfill, or not to fulfill? That is the question.

   No, it wasn't my fault. Whose fault is it for the way I was born? The doctor who delivered me, who hardly ever checked on my mom during labor – and she labored endlessly and in great pain – the doctor who ignored the heart monitor-probe that kept hitting my head while I was stuck in the birth canal during delivery? My grandma thinks so. But we don't know, we never pursued to prove it, so it's nobody's fault. It was just born with it and it somehow became part of me and the only thing I have to do is just to embrace it in all its beautiful, confusing glory, which sets off adventures that aren't to be planned out, and I just have to let them happen. That is another reason why I use a lot of metaphors from movies, books and television shows to help me understand reality as a whole, and why everything is meant to be. I know I don't live this illusion of thinking life is like a movie. It just helps me understand it more clearly. Also, it does help me to compare myself to characters in any movies, books and shows that'll help me give that confidence boost. I love to see a scenario, situation or person I can literally relate to or even just let me forget reality for some time.

## CHAPTER 14 - "I KNEW I'D GO BACK TO YOU" – SENIOR YEAR

Summer had ended and the school year was just beginning. Is it just me or is waking up on the very first day of me being a senior like being in a Rebecca Black music video?

It certainly felt like I reached an impossible milestone in my young adult life. The feeling of something different that had not been felt within me; something new and bold. I made myself breakfast and brushed my teeth. My grandma always said I was like clockwork, got up and got ready in the same sequence at the same time every morning and that start of school day was no different. I did the traditional thing that parents always do the very moment their kids head off to school: a first-day-of-school photo my grandma took of me rocking the outfit I'd chosen the night before, along with a few selfies. To me, it felt more important than the previous three years of my high school years, the fourth certainly felt special. I was also turning 18 that month.

I had my fair share of starting the new school year previously very weakly though I always had high expectations.

Now, I had the audacity, I made the high-standard promise for myself to start my fourth year, my senior year stronger than ever before. The kind of promise that felt more real and raw to me and that I had to fulfill. As if the earlier promises I've made in the past three years were like a flame on a candlestick, dead down after a single blow. But I felt the raging, burning sensation inside that my senior year was going to be different, more different, almost like a bonfire had been ignited withing me accelerating my own drives and ambitions.

  Every time I've started a new school year, the transition from summer to school almost felt unbearable. For me, it helped to give myself two weeks to fully get into the groove of a new school year, like a President with the First 100 days. It would not be a fair transition if both the students and teachers alike were to be dropped in an immediate adaptation without any adjustment whatsoever and it would drive me crazy. The first day and the first few days were always hard – after the daily swimming pool visits and the beach vacation and other summer trips had just ended. I had to accept with grace and not protest my own capability to get into the groove of daily class, to make it more comfortable on the long, winding road ahead. I was still in the General Education classes, I persevered in the classes where I truly belonged and felt that I had more to offer in a General Education class, testing my own knowledge.

  The teachers said the Standards of Learning (SOLs) will tell. Just because I'm autistic. Nothing like a good challenge.

After working with many tutors and taking other English classes and much practice with my aunt, I decided that I would finally be ready to take Mrs. Cruz English class again. Though I thought, 'oh no' with a groan, another spark ignited where a second chance, a second beginning began to blossom. I had learned there was no slacking off and my grandma had continuously checked the blackboard with me every day, standing behind me, making sure no more homework was missed. My autism wouldn't give me the upper hand, couldn't be used as a lame excuse but it would be the opposite, with a disability, I learned I would have to do the work and try to put much more effort into it – and I did.

As a junior the first time around in Mrs. Cruz class, English was so hard and I felt hopeless, and I never really wanted to feel that hopeless again, but I laid out the ground rules for myself to pass Mrs. Cruz's class.

This made my senior year a bit harder each day because of that little pact that I had made with my aunt, mom, grandma and myself to work harder and turn in every assignment in order to pass, not just the English classes, but all the classes.

My grandma was constantly reminding me of and checking on my homework, it was a daily drill.

When Mrs. Cruz started teaching the class, it was as if I had never taken it before. What she was saying actually was making sense; it was like a fog had lifted in the last year of all the tutoring and work my aunt had invested in me. I learned a lot in that English class, I took part and learned to understand the concepts and after a few weeks when Mrs. Cruz called on me, I knew the answers, and sometimes I was talking on endlessly. I could see pride in her eyes, pride for me? Pride for her teaching? There was no more awkwardness in the room.

And all the tutoring (paid tutors, my aunt and my grandma all tutored me) and all the associated pain was worth it. Toward the end of the class Mrs. Cruz wrote a letter to my grandma telling her how much better I'd become and so much different than the person she thought I was. So, my grandma and I gave Mrs. Cruz a book that my grandma wrote at the time about my great-grandfather during World War II and Mr. Cruz loved it so much. She exchanged many emails and phone calls with my grandma, and they became friends. And that also taught me that the very first impressions aren't always correct. She might have thought of me, again, as an unteachable or lazy kid. She assumed that a kid from the Special ED classes wasn't too fond of working extra hard to meet her expectations and just gave up when it was too challenging. It took a lot of work and help, and as my grandma always said, "it took a village," but finally I passed the class.

That second year of my junior year and the

senior year were a much more different time for me. I had finally learned to apply myself and put in the work, throwing myself into it and in the end, the bitter work, it was all worth it; it paid off.

And that all taught me, is that people whom you meet, or soon to meet will not be a one-way street. It'll be a highway with lots of interchanges that you don't go on.

And it is so true! The moral of the story of my little mishap with the English teacher is that I can also be the problem. It's me. I didn't do the work to prove to her that I could do the work. I didn't know any better. And yes, in the moment, it was awful and not laughable at all. In hindsight, I can just snicker at myself in self-deprecating humor that I wasn't a hard worker back then. But that now has changed.

High school has a hierarchy of class systems, in how the students treat each other – it is based and depends on their class levels and so many other things, like type of classes someone took, what they were in to, and their demographic. Like the class system in my most favorite science fiction book that was written in the early 1930s - "Brave New World" by Aldous Huxley. High school students treat each other based on what age and grade level they are in. For instance, freshmen are treated as if they are 'Epsilons' (fifth letter of the Greek Alphabet) because of how unsure they are of themselves, transiting from middle school. The sophomores are treated as if they are 'Deltas' (fourth letter of the Greek alphabet) because of how overconfident and overzealous. The juniors are treated as if they are both 'Gammas' (third letter of the Greek alphabet) and 'Betas' (second letter of the Greek Alphabet) because of how invested in their academic times they are, rather than hanging out with friends, almost like a Rory-Gilmore-vibe. The seniors, the top of the food chain, are treated as if they are 'Alphas' (first letter of the Greek Alphabet) because of how laid-back and relaxed they were, yet they still have to work hard in order to pass and graduate the entire class to go to that next step: college or the real world.

Each grade plays a role based on how successful they are, and many have different definitions of their own successes. Like how if a middle school student meets a high school student, there's a certain distant, disconnected blur line between what one thinks high school is like in the movies versus how the other side of the line sees a totally different model. Middle schools are like the 'Tales of Two Cities' always clashing with each other and high schools are more of a 'Brave New World' approach. This often helped me fit in, adapting to what ought to be adapted. But it's OK to view the world with rose-colored glasses if it helps to reflect and refract in said world. In moderation, it is good, but too much of that can have a toll on how you dictate your own reality from the things you read or watch.

# CHAPTER 15 – "YOU DON'T LOOK AUTISTIC"

The concept and idea of love and relationship had been absent and cut out for me throughout high school after the MacKenzie mishap which was a total rude awakening. The reason for that is because I don't want to waste my time, my devotions, my energies, and my breaths into something useless and meaningless - I had much bigger fish to fry than worrying about having a serious relationship, then having it dismantled by grownups.

I've slightly expanded my circle of friends since I've moved from the Special Education to General Education classes, especially in choir. I was easily approached by others and often told that I 'don't look autistic'. I definitely took that as a compliment, but what does an autistic look like? Not looking autistic, however, was how I was able to fit in with other non-autistic people. In my own mind, I don't see autistic and non-autistic just as when a president says that he doesn't see red states or blue states, in fact she sees the 'United States'. It's not a political statement on my part, it's just true, I don't care whether a person is autistic, I do care how that person carries him or herself without that autism label as a burden rather than a silver lining. But I don't critically look upon someone who doesn't carry themselves confidently. All I know is that we are all human beings with day-to-day routines and problems and stresses.

Autistic or non-autistic alike, we are all human beings.

The same but different in some ways.

And that is OK.

## CHAPTER 16 - A MAJOR MILESTONE

Even though I had that dramatic experience with MacKenzie, and I vowed to focus on myself and my education, I became friends with another girl. Well, it was more that she insisted to include me and talk to me. Her name was Madison and the first thing she told me was that she was adopted by her American single mother from China, after her parents had abandoned her as a few-days old newborn in front of a church. At the time, China only allowed one child per family and sadly her parents wanted a boy.

From the moment I met her, I truly admired her work ethic and how driven she really was. After a while, during class we became two peas in a pod. I also had a good work ethic; it was not as perfect as hers, but it was something. I would take notes and in case Madison didn't pay attention, she could review my notes. If I didn't understand the lecture, she would help me out.

She was definitely very different from MacKenzie. She seemed more intelligent and more driven and mostly more open. A bit hyper, but she was the kind of person who would crack a joke and had me snickering all the time. Madison said that she knew me during School-Age Child Care (SACC), the place my mom took me during elementary school for before- and after-care, because my mom got an important job.

It's somewhat amazing to meet someone the same age, who knew you from the beginning, the times when we were kids and when times felt simple, even though they really weren't; though I did not remember her from that time. I liked the way Madison viewed the world, adding insights to my own perspectives, uniting our viewpoints. For instance, I remember at the school cafeteria one day where Madison and another friend named Tom sounded like they were arguing, their perspectives clashing like two knights in an intense quarrel. I didn't intervene, but I just simply watched them as Tom was arguing with Madison saying that he simply had autism and couldn't help things that were out of his control. I was surprised to hear that Tom is also autistic, but he used it as a kind of shield of protection and as an excuse. I was sure that Madison knew that I too was autistic, but we had never talked about it. I believed that I carried myself as one who had goals, drive, and ambitions to fulfill and wouldn't let my own personal, inner struggles label me like a price tag nor a name tag. Stamped onto my chest: autistic. Yes, I know that I have something that I cannot control and would love to ask this question.

'You think that I wanted to be born like this?'

I would ask that question that doesn't need to be answered but to be looked upon with curiosity rather than frowned upon. The argument was very visible right in front of me and was a wake-up call blaring, buzzing and that since I knew Tom, I wanted to give my insights into what it meant to me to be an autistic person.

When Madison walked away to blow off steam, I chimed in with a friendly 'Hello' and Tom invited me with such delight. Seemed that he respected me, which gave me the green light to be sincere and open and honest.

"What was that about?" I asked.

Tom inhaled and exhaled, "Me and Madison are arguing."

"Oh, I can see." I chuckled, trying to lighten the mood, "So? What about?"

"About my own personal growth and struggles. I told Madison that I have autism and can't do anything about it; it's beyond my control," Tom said.

I thought about that for a bit. He sounded so helpless, but to me it felt like a pity excuse to walk through life covered in bubble-wrap, avoiding the clear, fresh water from a spring. Saying that Tom had autism was like a shield of protection for him, living in his own world and blocking the reality of possibilities that was in front of him.

"You know," I said, "Autism is just an intellectual disability. It's not meant to be a shield to make excuses for making and achieving the goals and dreams you have stored for your future. Look at me, I don't tell everyone I have autism, I don't wave it like a victim flag." I said it so sincerely.

Tom looked at me for a minute and then almost through me; He, at first frowned, then looked down in reconsideration, but he stayed quiet. I was worried how he would take my bold assertion, he could say, mind your own business, but to my surprise he said, "Well, maybe you're right." And thought about it some more, "No, you're absolutely right."

I could see the awakening look in his eyes. He nodded slowly, as if to let it sink in. "Maybe I need to put my own autism aside, not letting me be blocked by my own disillusion." He said it with such great intelligence, and it was like a light went on for him and for me as well, as if I were a guru, an autistic guru that gives pretty good and out-of-the-box insights on what it means to be autistic.

It's a fact that an intellectual disability is not meant to be a shield, but is the foundation to stand on to wake up every morning with renewed drive; not to forget your autism, but to forgive it in a way so I won't be so darn hard on myself when I'm not able to fulfill a task.

At the time in high school, I never really knew pride and self-reliance to effectuate my own destiny. But at that moment, a glimmer of pride started. I had made myself a teacher to Tom and told him to put his autism aside and to do the things most important to him but not to cancel himself, or to single out his autism as a burden, not to let it hold him back. That pride of mine at that moment talking to Tom was the size of a horse pill, hard to swallow, but gave me pleasure and immense, momentary fulfillment.

    I try to better my own capabilities by stretching the extent of what I'm capable of and I feel some compassion of someone who has autism, who dwells on it and blames it for all their bad experiences. It's not their fault that they were raised like that, and it is not my fault that I do what it takes, extending it. It was how I was raised and what is inside me that I became the way I am and I'm not blaming other people with autism - we have different forms of personal struggles that seem unclear to others.

    I'm almost pushing myself to the very limit and to the core. I'm like the type of person who would run up to a 15 feet tall wall, trying to get to the other side of it with my own powers. If it took me twenty times I would keep trying to be a much better version of myself, after completing the challenge. I was raised thinking there was nothing to blame, because despite my own autism, I was treated as if I weren't autistic. My family always said, whatever I put my mind to, I can try and try to achieve.

We tend to shield ourselves and people assume we don't face our issues that are worth dealing with. Sometimes, it is a good thing to be shielded, or to just shield myself from my own problems, but most days, I intend to take off that shield in order to confront my own problems.

Is it worth it to protect yourself from a world created specifically for people who don't have autism? Depending on the situation, yes, if a situation seems almost unbearable, it is OK to take a step back and just accept it as ' it's OK if you can't do anything given your own powers or abilities'.

Autistic or non-autistic, give yourself a break and don't overwork yourself to a point where you're hanging onto a thread.

I don't have to please everyone around me, but still have to blend into society while writing the rule paper the other way.

\*\*\*

Madison and I spent a lot of time together and our respect for each other grew more with each other, and no wonder others thought we were a couple. I didn't bring it up to her not because I didn't believe we could've been a great couple, but I was afraid of what she would say. Secretly I hoped I was more than just a great study buddy.

Then it came time for prom. Senior prom felt

more important, a watershed moment I had been looking forward to; an event that seemed impactful to my young adult life. I decided I would raise the question before my first ever, most important senior prom. I would ask Madison. It wasn't like Valentine's Day with the whole gift-giving debacle to MacKenzie when she turned on me as if I were a creep, it was more than that. I shuddered and was inspired when I finally saw the promposals in the building also posted to social media and thought of ways to make mine special. It would have to be heartfelt, but not like how social media influencers mock it as social status and gains for greater publicity.

    I confided in a class acquaintance, Sarah. When I told her I wanted to make a promposal for Madison, Sarah made it her life mission to make it possible. Days before the prom, after Government class I made my poster for Madison and Sarah guarded it until the perfect time. I had to leave the cafeteria early to get ready before Madison could spot me. I was in full-on Pink Panther-mode. In the hallway, I sprinted to the government class room to be ready when Madison arrived there. The trick for something special to happen is to keep it low-key, almost like setting up a harmless prank of putting toothpaste in an Oreo and being subtle, like a spy infiltrating into the villain's secret lair. I could not give it away with a facial expression hinting at something being up. I was ready. I waited in the class room for her to arrive.

I still remember that very moment when Madison walked into the government classroom and saw me holding the sign and Sarah recorded it on her phone.

Madison's face lit up and her eyes got so big the moment she saw me there with the sign and of course immediately knew what it meant and what it was for.

She said "yes" in a high pitch and ran up to me to hug me. This was going a lot better than my Valentine's Day fiasco.

Of course, we had our photo and video together for Instagram to jump on the Prom social media bandwagon. For me, outwardly I didn't try to brag that I'm going to Prom with Madison, I kept it modest and humble. But inward I wanted to scream with excitement. That was the proudest moment in my whole senior year - the highlight of it all.

\*\*\*

Prom finally came. The night all seniors dream of, this very magical night, even the whole preparations of it all were exciting. I got dressed in my one perfect tuxedo, which luckily, I already had from my choir class. All week and especially the afternoon of prom I anticipated the night. Butterflies shuddered my stomach wildly and gleefully. It was for me until then the most memorable day to anticipate and to prepare for; what is called 'the night to remember'. Watching teen dramas where older actors and actresses dressed as teenagers that showed scenes and montages of them getting ready for Prom is the only media that got it correct fairly close of how we young people truly anticipate the night of inclusivity, a positive rite of passage for us to dance the sparkling, twinkling night away. All our dreams burn bright, sniffed out from darkness in blazing, blinding lights.

 My aunt decorated my grandma's car with twinkling lights inside and they both chauffeured us to our first destination: Taking pictures.

 My mom and dad, aunt and grandma snapped beautiful shots of me, the first-born and Madison, both of us all Gatsby 'ed-up, out in the wilderness near a creek, somewhere majestic before our 'hakuna matata' night was about to unfold. It felt like paparazzi were ascending on us.

 After the photos - my aunt had helped me book a restaurant – my grandma and aunt drove me there to grab a bite to eat before burning the calories on the dance floor. I felt incredibly special with Madison the moment she and I walked into the restaurant with our prom outfits on, feeling almost invincible, not in a self-absorbed kind of way. It was nice to sit in a leather booth and to see what was on the menu. I was like an adult male at the age of thirty trapped inside an eighteen-year-old body.

"This is nice." Madison said, admiring the tone and atmosphere of the restaurant: The dimmed lighting, the faint sounds of chatting people and clashing utensils, pots, and pans with the aromas that flooded the air with savory and crispy scents. I nodded, couldn't agree more. It was magnificently beautiful and charming, like the restaurant scene in the teen romance 'The Fault in Our Stars' but without the bubbly champagne. I didn't need the champagne to fully capture the magic of pre-Prom dinner, I only needed a substitute for champagne: mineral water in a champagne glass. As we ordered our meals, of course we got the usual: cheeseburgers, as if this were at Five Guys, but it certainly felt like a fancy restaurant. We were growing teenagers after all and we didn't really need fancy, rich-people meals to fill our bellies before hitting the dance floor.

We ordered our meals and also saw another student from our government class, and he too was going to Prom with a girl I had never met. Both Madison and I were surprised that someone else from our school would be at that same low-key restaurant, almost astonished. We waved at them, but they ignored us, pretending not to even know us, and we carried on with our own food, drinks and each other's company. I just cared that he was also going to Prom and nothing else. Above all, prom nights are supposed to be the magical night where all surrounding worries melt away like chocolate, because prom is like a box of chocolates, (ya know the rest to that).

    Admiring, breathing the savory, fresh, and crisp air of the best times of our lives. We munched, we laughed, we snapped cutesy, artsy photos, chatted. Prom was something good for high school seniors – we felt like we were in our late twenties, growing up a little too fast, but we embraced it instead of fighting the process. I think it was all worth the stress of endless rabbit holes of homework to get to the end of the dark tunnel because now we got the reward of prom, letting the stress of the past be past, to enjoy the precious times like Gollum with the Rings.

    After cleaning off the plates, I waved my hand to the waiter for the check. Now, I felt even more grown. Waving up my hand as if I were in my mid-twenties after meeting with an old friend of mine, waving my hand to impress that old friend of mine - how self-reliant I've grown to be. I used my grandmother's credit card, respectfully, paid just for the meals, not anything else and learned to tip the waiter, not because of my good, amazing mood but to just be generous. After paying for the delicious meals, we headed out the door, waved 'goodbye' and 'see ya there' to our government class buddy, despite him still ignoring us, to go to the location where the actual prom was taking place.

*** 

We arrived at where the prom took place, and it was a nice, fancy Marriott hotel.

My grandma drove us to the hotel with my aunt in the front passenger seat, Madison and I in the back being chauffeured. We enjoyed the little twinkly lights, it all felt festive.

We pulled into the front where the other kids in their fancy prom outfits were snapping photos for the 'gram. Madison and I climbed out of the car like a couple of Class-A actors, never mind the car was a Toyota Corolla - but we walked down the red carpet while the camera shuttered twenty miles an hour and the flashes almost blinded us. Prom was definitely like the Oscars, or any of those prestigious award shows where actors, actresses, directors and so-ons walked down the soft red carpet, striking poses in front of camera and reporters screaming out at them for their own stories for their news sources.

But our prom of course wasn't that prestigious, just a magical, glamorous night we kids dreamt of when we were younger. Going to prom had melted away my own autism, as if I didn't have it at all. And the only thing, I did admire about my prom was how special and pampered I felt. It was like being thrown in a blender with the other mixed berries and fruits in the most amazing ways, and we were all the same; I didn't have to work as hard as usual to try to fit into the crowd, it just felt natural that I belonged right then and there for this one night. In all my four years, I've felt alienated due to my own autism and had to work hard to fit into the crowd of different types of people, but prom night, no siree, no stress whatsoever. I fit in like I was no longer an outcast, as if I stepped into that prom as if I weren't autistic. I was me.

Entering the lobby, there was a crowd of other ritzy dressed kids talking, laughing, and just living through this marvelous moment in their lives. Giving our tickets and walking deeper some more to soak it all in, like Alice opening the doors to Wonderland, it felt like all the stress was worth this reward in the end.

In my fancy tux, it felt like I was floating in a bed of stars with a gentle tone running through my brain. The stresses of those four years of my life were just a long, long dark tunnel and this very moment as a senior was the light at the end of it all. Those dark hours of those times in high school where I was the light, the little engine that kept on going. Despite my own autism, my own learning capabilities that came with great struggles, I continued to push through and got to enjoy my own magical prom night, like the other non-autistic students.

I danced the night away until the sun came up – it was the most magical night.

***

Soon it was time to walk with my peers in a cap and gown with the biggest grin on my face. It was roughly four days after that magical prom, and it was the weeks of preparation when the big day arrived. Graduation. That primal light to that dark tunnel.

A stepping stone. A milestone. A moment.

A moment that felt that it needed to be celebrated as I prepared for the road ahead of me. To me, it was a big, big deal to walk down the graduation yellow brick road with my navy-blue gown as if it were a cape, or the clothing of an Air Nomad, from "Avatar: The Last Airbender." I've dreamt of the day when I could physically walk down that aisle and felt super confident while doing it. Not treating me like I was on a runway in some chic Fashion Week, I was not representing the cap and gown, I was representing myself in reaching that primal achievement. It's empowering to look back from the past in great awe and glee at the person I've become today - looking back onto that long, winding road traveled by, in retrospect it was a mountain traveled through.

The day before graduation, that hot June in

2018, butterflies shuddered my belly wildly, anticipating. Who would've thought the day before graduation was so nerve-wracking? Well, it was nerve-racking, because it was the ending point to that long, long, winding road that led through a rocky mountain and finally, I was on a flat, plain road - a straight one. Me sitting in a nearby Starbucks, both admiring and nervous for the day of my graduation and vowing myself I wouldn't get so worked up.

    I thought, "this is good. What are you worried about? You made it to the end, the turning point. Luckily you don't have to give a speech." Although it would be cool yet even more nerve-racking to speak to the entire Class of 2018 like I did at my final choir performance when I had to speak in front of the entire choir and family audience. I along with the others in choir one by one had to introduce ourselves and list our future plans, which school we would be attending; goals and more. I stood up there on the podium and spoke in front of dozens of people. After the choir ceremony when I was reunited with my family, I noticed that all their eyes were very red, and they all said how proud they were of me.

    But for graduation, no I didn't have to give a speech. Yet it was still daunting whether to present or not, it was the day of myself in a navy-blue cap and gown with the tassel of the year '2018' on it walking in front of hundreds - it just had to be perfect.

Perfect may even seem like an illusion, but still I wanted it to be.

***

Excitement took over me, squelching the worry, so I needed to decide what I wanted to wear. I decided on a crisp white dress shirt, cream-colored khaki pants, and an orange tie. I wanted my graduation attire to match my own school colors. The gown was, of course, navy-blue and it ran through my mind that together with the orange tie it looked like a turned-up light bulb. A-ha, jackpot, bingo!

The ceremony was at nine in the morning on a Saturday and I got up a bit earlier to shower and to get ready for that big day. I wanted all the worry to melt away like white chocolates in the summer sun with the only thing left standing my pride and excitement. I never imagined as a middle-schooler or a freshman of high school that the hours before the whole graduation ceremony would be so alarmingly restless. I just love to wonder, letting my mind wander, how my younger self would have reacted to my present self, all nervous and worried, like a time-traveler who made a longtime journey to the post-Kindergarten years. In some ways my younger self would be astonished, that I mustered all my energy into being in the classes I wanted to be and proven the teachers wrong, who didn't think I could. I used my own powers, like pumping oil into a squeaky, rusty machinery.

I got into my graduation attire and my grandma and aunt zoomed me to the arena and I hopped out of the car to be around with my other peers. My aunt Ingrid came with me just to stand with me to calm my nerves and to make sure I got into my line, which teachers organized alphabetically by names. When it was time to get ready, Ingrid wished me good luck and told me that I would do great. She then left to go to the arena to join my mom, dad, brother, sister, and grandma, ready to snap some photos of my snazzy outfit, both for Instagram and for our memory to frame.

In line we waited and waited. Finally, after more than an hour of organizing, organizing, and I don't know, more organizing, we finally started moving, like from a tight traffic jam to the speed of sixty zooming onto the highway. From a small, narrow hall that connected to the main arena, I walked like a superhero, who rebelled against policies on Edna Mode's views on capes - yes, capes are double-edged swords; they make you feel super empowered, yet they also could get caught in anything.

We got to the main arena with the faint "Pomp and Circumstance Graduation Walking

March" in the air. Walking in the middle of the arena was so surreal yet almost dream-like, and I was in-and-out of a dream.

*Is it really happening?* I thought and was mentally pinching myself, not knowing whether it was a dream or not. For me, walking in the middle of the arena was like a living, breathing example of a Theodore Roosevelt speech. Not a soul who can just point out from the distance how a 'strong man stumbles' or 'where the doer of deeds could have done better.' 'The credit belongs to the man who is actually in the arena.' All those four years were intense, but I had shown with a lot of diligence that there were no shortcuts in my own great successes. I only had one small hurdle to overcome. I didn't pass the final Reading SOL test, which because of my autism I could finish as a super senior. I'm a strong reader, but I feel that the reading SOL problems are so tricky, and my autistic brain often misses the nuances, but my family was convinced with some tutoring I could pass. There were times I wasn't so sure.

Still, this didn't stop me from walking and getting my Applied Studies Diploma. I got to walk with my Highschool peers and "graduate" with them. Those four years helped make me the person I am therefore, the credits belonged to me and my aunt who studied more with me than anyone; all my tutors and good teachers; my mom who started my individual education plans from early on and went to every single IEP meeting and of course my grandma, the rock.

    I deserved this more than anything in the universe. No matter what the universe has in store for me, I'm willing to take it on diligently. When I got my Applied Studies Diploma pressed into my proud hands, I didn't do those crazy things like a backflip in victory. It was more of a John Bender who yanked his fist into the air in the Breakfast Club movie.

    It's like writing a letter to Mr. Vernon, from the movie, about how I accepted the fact that I had to sacrifice an entire whole four years of my life with the constant reminder of what I had to prove to the naysayers. But I thought he's crazy for making me write a letter telling him who the F I am. He sees me as he wants to see me - in the simplest form, in the most convenient definition. But I found out that I'm the kind of person who was given a rule paper to write the other way from the standard or given a coloring page to color either in or outside the lines.

    Does that answer your question?

    Sincerely yours, me.

## CHAPTER 17 - THE MARVELOUS NEXT PHASE

"Back At It Again, Without Any White Vans"

You would've thought I was done with high school after the standard four years. You thought I was off the hook, off to college or vocational/tech school as my marvelous, next phase.

No, that wasn't the case. Besides still needing to pass the English reading SOL, my kryptonite, I had to attend an additional fifth year to finish up some other classes I did not complete during my four years. Because I walked with my Class of 2018 peers, I remained a member of Class of 2018 who had to make up one year to get a full High School Diploma, which my mom insisted I get, since in her mind "there would be so many more job opportunities," if I had a full High School Diploma.

Another mountain and a long, winding road slowly formed but I wanted to again start the climb.

And so, the struggle continued....

At first when I found out that I would be held back and having to do another school year I thought it was a bad thing, but my family reminded me that considering the diagnosis of Dr. Ophelia when I was a baby I did incredibly well. I got to walk with my Class of 2018 peers and that's been planted into the soils of my brain and now turned into a magnificent garden. It's been marinating in my memories.

    To continue as a super senior was the decision the school board made for me and my folks, aunt and grandma and I agreed and accepted. It wasn't made by any of the teachers who wanted to bring me down, down from my own past successes . It was made by the few educators, who wanted what's best for me because they had seen me sprout up like a weed, physically, socially and academically. They all agreed I could go all the way and get this full High School Diploma. Probably, my freshman self would resent me for having to keep going another year but my current self would have to heartfeltly explain to my former, younger self that there will be decisions made that seem annoying or even unfair and outside of my control or capabilities but there is always a silver lining behind the larger scheme of things. That was my mantra for this fifth year to focus on the silver lining to overcome the times that may seem the darkest. That was my beacon. That would explain it all to my own younger self, visiting from a time portal. It also helped to know that I wouldn't be the only super senior. Madison also needed to take another year to finish, but she had big goals: she would go to community college; her main challenge: she had ADHD, and it was hard for her to focus.

    We talked a lot. Explained to each other that there are so many good things in this world but we only harness and focus on the negatives, taking all the good things we have for granted. Not truly embracing how things really are, such as it was a decision made by others, not a choice by us to do a fifth year. Not to just throw away what my younger self had been striving for, but to harness a new kind of drive.

    While attending that high school all those years, I felt as if I was a prince living in a castle with several acres of land outside but when you reached the end there was a seventy-foot wall. I truly believe that all the things I've learned through textbooks and history books make the world feel so grand, but the actual world is not that. What is beyond those books? Beyond the castle, beyond the seventy-foot wall? high school taught me so much and I felt more comfortable and confident there, like a prince soaking up all his royalties. Yet still when looking out of the window, looking beyond, like I was in a Disney song, I wasn't sure that I could go the distance, but I was hoping I'll get there someday.

    Now officially done with high-school and just being a "super senior," the journey on a new road to a new destination started. This time, it wasn't about fighting for my own worth in this world as an autistic person but to truly find my own worth as an individual.

Looking out the window was now self-discovery.

~

In my super senior year, there was a program I was assigned to which was supposed to help students with any kind of disabilities learn about office-setting and -etiquettes. A two-credit course that would help students like me make informed career decisions and continued education choices as we transition from school to the work force; a program that helps young students to adapt to a workplace environment and possibly the norms of society. The program took place in a secondary school, Mayfield Secondary School.

I attended the program along with my longtime friend from elementary school and two that knew me since Pre-K, Wyatt and Constance. Wyatt and I have the same kind of thought process, but he is more of a prankster and Constance was in the Special Education classes but doesn't really know better and you can't blame her. She's kind of like a female version of Theodore Decker from a Donna Tartt book "The Goldfinch" where I'm walking alone in a school hallway and out of nowhere, she pulls me into a room to chat endlessly. And I will not get a word in, not that it matters to her. But I do respect that Constance viewed me as if I were her idol during her time in middle school. I was in the same Special Education class during my awkward middle school days, and I bet she daydreamed to reunite with me when she got to high school. She did, because she remembered me since we were yay-high at a local daycare place at a playground, especially at the sandbox. I do believe however, that Constance idolizes me too much, expecting the same little boy from the sandbox, not realizing that changes had kicked in and sprouted me up like a weed. She knows little of the long, winding road I've traveled which made me who I'm in the present: a bit reluctant to trust people. But I feel that somebody like Constance has a hard time accepting change and wants to stay and keep things as they are.

    Changes are inevitable.

    They are going to happen whether you like it or not. Autistic or not, great, greater, or even the greatest of all changes are soon to happen, sooner or later. Treat them as a positive version of a premonition, not to hide in denial but to let the true changes mold you, adjust to it. This I won't ever say to Constance because of how self-conscious I'm about sounding condescending: "I'm no longer that guy you knew in the sand box." That's the only thing I like about my own autistic self, it made me a very, very self-conscious person and I put my own needs aside to help others. I would never want to hurt anyone's feelings, ever. Autism is a spectrum of all different types of people in the pot of the autism soup, it's not just that you could throw in the R-word, adding to the ingredients. It's not a disability that is only burdensome but look for the blessing in disguise. Why try to abolish it? Try to study more of it, study more of the 'ables' in the 'labels'. It made us who we are, it made me who I'm and society raise the bar super high on the expectations they put on us like a scroll still rolling out a thousand miles away. We have our own standards that keep us striving and thriving all the steps of the way, some would be harder to bear. It's OK if a task seems harder at first in your own head than in reality, which happens to me a lot. For instance, doing homework or doing the dishes at first seemed like climbing Mount Everest in which even the smallest number of dishes and or papers piled up overwhelmed me. But over time, slowly but surely, I took it one piece at a time, starting small first and then the big plates and bowls. Society intends to lay out what is expected by someone with autism as if we aren't the way we are and we do get ashamed if we act abnormally from the other billions of people in the world.

*But what is normal?*

Like it is our fault to be born this way, which it is not. The only problem society lays out and the internal struggles we have brewing inside is that society often doesn't easily accommodate any living, breathing human being that happens to have autism.

Accommodate, not to coddle us to make society light and fluffy, you don't need to baby-proof the sh*t out of us but to make it better and easier for us to keep up rather than to hinder.

Some autistic people that are non-verbal and in wheelchairs are the greater exceptions and do have the right to favors, because they greatly need them and it is not their fault they were born that way, so leave your ableism aside in order to do someone a good deed. I'm not saying that this program all the teachers weren't supportive, some had good beliefs, like that we are living, breathing human beings that don't need to be fixed but to be adjusted to accommodate ourselves to society.

*But when will society adjust to us?*

One of the teachers in the program was named Sylvie Jamie, so we called her "Ms. Jamie". She was the kind of teacher in the EFRW program who actually saw that I had some potential, had so much to offer, and brought something to the table. She listened, let me speak without interrupting me and did not talk over me, as if I didn't have a single notion of what I'm talking about. I always anticipate how they talk to me or about me and I know that there's a difference being talked over or having a conversation.

Please let an autistic person say what they have to say, what's on their mind and just listen and not snatch that microphone before we can finish our thoughts.

      Ms. Jamie definitely believed that autism is on a spectrum, an infinity or a Pi symbol that goes on forever and ever. She was strict on office etiquettes but you would have to be a bit strict and need some kind of a pep talk to be able to grab an invisible sledgehammer to tear down that wall that'll prevent you from chasing down your own goals and dreams that'll lead to your own happiness. I don't have a broken piece missing within, I'm infinity, linked to something wholesome and unique and Ms. Jamie saw that that I had potential. My biggest goal was to mold all the other things that are positive about me, instead of calling myself autistic - some areas made me feel a bit uncomfortable at the time. Uncomfortable in a way that you wear tight skinny jeans or a nice suit that you want to quickly change into something more comfortable after a long day and night. Calling myself autistic was a 'love/hate' thing, some days I would wear it like a banner, or a scarlet letter stamped on my chest that shouted out my identity, some other days I wanted to just tossed it to the inferno. That I do believe that I do have potential and have more to offer than just calling myself, declaring that I have something that I was diagnosed to since I was yay-high. I had that mentality to prove to others that I could work harder and constantly astonishing both myself and the surrounding people, which was how I taught my brain, my inner fibers, my internal flames. That was my drive, my momentum, the gas that kept pumping. I was an optimist, and I believe that there are good people with good intentions, people like Ms. Jamie who just wanted the absolute best for me. Programs like the EFRW had good intentions, great ways of wisdom to help somebody like me without revealing themselves as the opposites - spiteful leeches that suck the lives out of us, contradicting it another, disguising it as good, charitable things.

  There are good people in the world that help out people like me to make them understand a brave, cruel world that made it hard to fit in.

  ~

  One of the most cherished memory I have being in this super-senior program was after a few months of getting into the groove of the program I was invited to spend time with fourth graders and to help out the librarian in the North Westchester Elementary school. This memory so dear to my heart, and I hold it so tightly and I will never let go. The reason why I cherish this time is because I got to read to elementary school students. They listened to me with big eyes and never judged. I could never read enough to them; their brains were like sponges, and they wanted to hear more and more. In my viewpoint looking at young kids is seeing the future in front of my very eyes, and it was my responsibility to be a vessel somehow, a kind, gentle person to those kids. And they needed a figure such as myself and I wanted to be a kind example to these kids. Sometimes I let the kids read to me, slowly putting the letter together, forming words, I could help them by being patient and not pulling away the book if they weren't fast enough. I showed the kids patience that I so often longed for from my teachers.

There I also got to help out at the library and worked with the nice librarian Mrs. Moyer and also got to help out with the cafeteria ladies, their welcoming smile made my heart grow three times its size and made me a new, wholesome, and much better version of myself.

This super-senior semester working with the elementary school kids who had no inkling that I was autistic and looked at me admiringly and in great anticipation, along with working in the library was one of my very favorite times there.

*"Vessel"*

*"...But a role model in the flesh provides more than inspiration; his or her very existence is confirmation of possibilities one may have every reason to doubt, saying, 'Yes, someone like me can do this'."*
*~ Sonia Sotomayor*

~

This elementary school program led to my own personal growth and discoveries about my true self. I always knew that I was great with kids, and it was because I have three younger siblings - a little brother and by now I also had two little sisters who shaped me into a totally different person. There were days before I became an older brother, I did feel appalled when I'd hear kids at a mall throwing fits, laying on the ground kicking and screaming. At that time, I would get annoyed and possibly scowled. But after my little brother Theodore was born, that changed and rearranged every cell, every fiber of my body and I just knew that I have to be an older brother, a figure to this second-born that was brought into this world.

Now, I see kids at the mall or at the supermarket and I truly feel for them and understand that it is hard to be kids as well as being a kid with autism. Especially being a kid with autism. For me, I had some discord memories as a kid where I felt alienated yet not really being attached to this earth, like I was constantly in a state of a dream world and according to Constance where she remembered me when I was a kid and even a bit non-verbal. She told me repeatedly that she would kick the sand in the sandbox at a local daycare, not to my face but to my direction and I would say a sound, but not a word, like 'stop'. She would cackle, crack up with that little nugget of a story about me as a child and somehow, I do feel that she sort of envied me in how I had changed in those years, from that kid in the sandbox to the man I'm today. As if she is frozen in time, like a vampire, ageless while people surrounding her ought to grow up, inevitably.

Slowly but surely, that could and would be Constance's painful rude awakening like an old inflatable waiting to burst in place of a new one. Walt Disney would say, 'growing old is mandatory, but growing up is optional.'

Growing old is certainly inevitably, inescapably bound to happen, it's predetermined and predestined. But you certainly don't have to give up your own innocence in order to grow up as an adult, in Walt Disney's case, he was saying that 'growing up is optional' but don't pull a Peter Pan. We all are kids at heart, but we can't be manchildren that form inflatables that alter what is really reality, shielding us otherwise and live in full denial. For instance, I keep my little nuggets of my own childhood photos in a photo album, but I don't want to be the same as I once was . Yes, I was that boy on the sandbox who didn't know how to speak in full-sentences, but somehow, I'm not that boy now, but only could recall that in the dusty, wrinkly parts of my brain of what were the 'good ole days' of my life.

That was why I enjoyed my time there at the

North Westchester Elementary School, not to have a total recall of my own youth but to see myself in those kids. I'm sure any kid who looks at an adult or a teenager thinks that they never once were kids themselves, thinks we were surrogate to adulthood without going through childhood and adolescence. Not to be judgmental toward how kids frown upon an adult who once used to be a kid, but it could be baffling but it's true: adults once were also kids themselves in different time zones and periods. Even though nowadays there are handheld phones and social media, the older adults once were kids before advanced technology, but the childhood memories were somehow the same as if a kid nowadays despite the technology changes.

~

Being in a classroom of fourth graders and those small, blue, plastic chairs that made me felt like a giant - listening with open arms, curious eyes, and an admired open heart in how those fourth graders read so fluently. Sometimes I would either listen to them read or play a fun game of Uno or Connect-Four, even though I was older and a bit stiff doesn't mean I could not have fun. It impressed me how smart those kids were and also how relatable they were. Just because they were fourth graders, doesn't mean I couldn't relate to them.

I do remember when I helped out in the cafeteria in the elementary school, I encountered two adorable kindergartens who finally saw somebody a bit younger. The most adorable were two who lured me to them just to mess with me, almost like in that stand-up special I had watched before on Netflix where the comedian, Taylor Tomlinson, discussed never falling for the trap of interacting with a baby. Yet it was so adorable and possibly those two little boys had rarely seen somebody as young as I was and just wanted to have some fun. They were kids after all and you can't really control all aspects of a kid, but it is good to lay out rules for them (I know, it does sound a bit contradictory).

  I'm sure when days before I set foot into the school, those two little boys just were told in a huff scowl to 'eat their lunches'. This was an exception when they saw me in the center of the cafeteria, watching to see if any kids needed a napkin, packets of ketchup, or in case they spilled something. They would giggle and by raising their hands, lure me toward them then playfully laughing in my face. Because they're kids who just wanted to have some fun and who would have blamed them. Never blame a kid for being a kid.

  ~

  The EFRW program was the kind of program

that was perfect for any young people who happen to be neurodivergent. It was down-to-earth sort of program where I could look back and appreciate Ms. Jamie's good intentions into remodeling, reshaping what is beyond that wall in my own little universe. I could look back now seeing the North Westchester Elementary School with that smile that cannot be wiped off my face. When you let in the right people with the right kind of intentions, anything is possible and don't really scowl, or frown.

      I just knew that program was just one year, but the best one year of my life that I would never change for the world. It's good to have good representations of what being autistic really comes to be and also, to have the right kind of people with the right hearts at the right time. To also prepare people like me in how not only to fit to society but play along the lines, like an actor reading off the script. For me, it's OK to be given a ruled paper to have the sudden urge to write the other way, but do subtly so that people won't be scared. In theory, people don't really think about you the way you think about yourself in a way that grade school taught. Again, there is a blurred line that cannot be crossed, and if crossed, people have to make rational decisions. Rationality seems necessary, but how on earth do we know what blurred line not to cross and for what inevitably could happen? You just have to know by control. In order to know that blurred line, knowing it cannot be crossed due to insanity.

Mentally and spiritually know which is that blurred line. It'll be hard to find which is the one, but you would know soon enough when that has been crossed with the help of stressed with fear facial expressions of bystanders.

Again, it is good that programs like the EFRW program exist to help out people like me that need more guidance, some new set of skills to learn to survive the jungle of a real world. To strip away my own autism and yours, we are all human beings just trying to keep the body and soul together without being totally ripped to shred. To add autism back onto the masses, we are all human beings that are unique in our own abilities that make us unique. Sadly, it was just one year with the EFRW program, and it remains logged to my memories forever.

~

Autism shouldn't be discarded nor removed, stripped away from us in which it sort of made us the people who are. It's just that the world isn't made for people like me, not to adjust to accommodate so we comfortably fit in without having a crazed sensory overload. It should be woven into so gently, so easily like a new, fresh thread into the mass of a soft quilt. Not so much of a puzzle piece, because it has implied to the autism community as 'broken', 'a piece missing', and that we cannot live happy, fulfilling lives. Autism is a spectrum, not something to frown upon in disarray, it is a unifying thing to realize that it is not a bridge from one side to the next, yet it is a bridge that goes on and on that doesn't seem to have an ending point.

What goes on and on is the journey itself.

A journey still has not been discovered, in the process.

## PART II - FIRST EXPERIENCE

*"It's like we never even happened / Baby, what the F is up with that? (Huh) /And good for you, it's like you never even met me." ~ Song "good 4 u" by Olivia Rodigo*

## CHAPTER 18 – REVELATION

*"But if I'm being honest / I miss you / But I hate you at the same time / You broke your promise / Now I don't know / What was real or a lie / If I'm being honest I don't want to let go / But I fell in love with someone that I don't know / If I'm being honest."* ~ song *"If I'm Being Honest"* by Anna Clendening

You remember that one other revelation I had with my high school crush on Valentine's Day? It happened again during the Class of 2019 senior prom when I decided to go to a second prom with a friend of mine, Wyatt. A rude awakening, another revelation had struck within me like a lightning bolt and that had me completely awake.

A new season rolled in after the cold, dead of winter: spring and for the new seniors to get ready for their last days of high school. The anticipation of prom and graduation again was in the air. I smiled reminiscing how I felt during that time of my own prom and graduation.

My times as a super senior were also very memorable and special because of the friendship I had with Madison to me felt even stronger. She and I hung out all the time. For instance, we would go to a nearby Starbucks or to a Kung Fu Tea place where I tried my first bubble tea and we would just sit and talk and joke around, like any other young people. Definitely a spark had ignited between me and Madison, because of course she knew me from the times of when we were little, and we were study buddies, and we were like the ying and the yang.

My friend Wyatt was going to his prom and invited me to go along with him, but he also needed a female date. At first, I had some skepticism about going to a second prom, which could imply that I had not gotten over my own milestone yet.

After Wyatt invited me, I didn't decline at that very moment but did the classic 'I'll think about it' bit. I was not the kind of person who immediately declined, yet I wanted to think about whether I would accept the invitation. I didn't want to go to a different class's prom as if I wasn't yet done with my own, as if it were in a video game completing a level I had already beaten. I thought long and hard about it, yet I loved to dance and to have a good time, but my own skepticism about not really knowing many in that class kept getting in the way of me being excited about it.

"What the heck," I said a few days later, "I'll go, but you'll still need a female date, right?"

"Madison is going with me," Wyatt said.

"Madison? My Madison?" I asked, I felt a knot in my stomach.

"Yes, she said she'd go with me." He shrugged.

I needed to talk to Madison. It was the night before Valentine's Day, I already had picked out a nice necklace for her.

When I got home, she waited for me on my front door steps so we could hang out together.

"What to get some bubble tea?"

"Wyatt said you're going to prom with him?"

"Yes, I am." She looked at me, "I just want to make sure that everyone has a prom date. Nobody should go to prom alone, especially someone like Wyatt, another autistic person. Out of all people you should understand."

I can recall that moment as clear as the waters at Cancún, Mexico and how that statement rocked my world. Rocked it as the Richter scale would measure the 2011 Washington, DC 5.8 earthquake, which was how badly my world was rocked.

I said I had to do some more homework.

"I can work with you."

"No, it's OK." I walked inside and shut the door.

It all didn't really sink in until the morning when my grandma and I further discussed it and the more it creeped in and the more I let it soak in, I felt foolish. I realized that I had been her community project; I had been her charity. How could I've thought for one minute to be anymore to her? I had imagined us kissing at some point soon.

But…., I'm autistic. Her reasons for hanging out with me were completely different than I had envisioned.

Her going to prom with Wyatt motivated me to no longer talk to her. I made up my mind that I was going to my second prom, to Wyatt's first prom, while Madison was going to prom with Wyatt.

***

Seconds became minutes, minutes became hours, days became weeks, and we didn't talk. I avoided Madison by not texting her; in school we would ignore each other. My thoughts would often spiral; the whole thing felt plastic and fake and the way she had treated me, so nice and kind, but for the wrong reasons. I had feelings for her, but she always had me in the friendzone; the autistic friend she needed to be nice to. I was naïve to think she wanted more.

*Could I ever find love, even in my own nongregarious ways? Would I ever find love the way I'm without being painfully ostracized as if I was an abomination?* I didn't want to be the pity friend. Maybe I knew deep, deep-down Madison didn't see me as a boyfriend, but I had been very hopeful. I was told that people in the autism spectrum are really nice, too nice that we don't really see the cunning ways and the deception of people as easily, which I find horrible how we autistic people don't really see that side of people immediately, we only see the aftermath of it. Like we are all blind in our own kindness and tenderness that deceptive people step in so deviously sneakily and dishonest. It's not our fault that we are born the way we are born.

Born nice. Born kind.

No blame, no shame to be born the way we are, so that others could step in to reach to our pockets and tug on our hearts without even noticing; a hug that seems meaningful but it's meaningless, a pity hug. Me sitting on my bed, or on a couch, staring at my phone, expecting to text Madison back, to talk to her like old times, but my scornful resentment crept up to slap my hand from even touching my phone.

Remembering what she did and not to give in.

Days became weeks, weeks became months. Not texting Madison back almost felt childish but yet I still felt the same amount of indignation I felt at the beginning of this rude awakening. The more I sat and thought bitterly about Madison, the more happy memories of our prom and our own graduation pictures, or photos of us at a coffee shop talking and laughing turned from color to stale black-and-white and fuzzy. The perception that I had planted in my mind about all the time I had spent with Madison, now evaporated. Although, it felt like it vaporized but it was still logged into my brain pushing aside the thought of 'look at the positives and all the fun times you had with Madison' to kind of exclude these thoughts to, now, the resentment that had shaped and molded into the new narrative. I knew that Madison had a pretty unpleasant childhood, but it doesn't excuse her behavior; nobody wants a pity friend. What happened in her past is in the past, and any kind of trauma that happened then isn't an excuse for her current behavior. From then on, I told myself over and over again that the only person you know is you. Not have to depend on other people to fix any meaningful or meaningless conundrums and for me, as a neurodiverse person, it is my true dislike to be dependent on others and their feelings, their behaviors, their emotions, because that I know deep down that if I show any vulnerability of being dependent, it can be misused. I do know the difference between asking for help and being dependent on others, and I will never want to be dependent on others again. I never want to be at the mercy of their behavior again.

    There's this love-hate thing about being a neurodiverse because it makes me who I'm but also limits my true abilities in how I want to conduct things. Like a conductor who conducts a whole orchestra, and no music or tunes comes out.

    People may not understand, but don't get into a tizzy whether they look or frown upon us somehow silently and with hidden disrespect. They may not understand what autism is nor grasp the correct terminology; it just takes more time for other closed-minded neurotypicals to open that metal vault door. Not even Toph, from Nickelodeon's "Avatar: The Last Airbender" could metal-bend that metal vault.

~

    I accepted my invitation to go Wyatt's prom. Madison at that point declined going to prom with Wyatt to avoid any further damaging conflict.

    It was probably for the best that we let the raging flame between us sizzle out peacefully rather than constantly patting out the flames. It was still very new for me to learn Madison's true colors, it was a big adjustment losing her as a close friend, and maybe she never had the intention to mentally sabotage and hurt me; she was just never at the same stage I was. My expectations were different than what she was ever willing to provide.

    It's also my own perception that took the steering wheel of my own mind as a strong motivation to not forgive her. Over and over again I was thinking of being mentally stabbed in the back and the scar is still there in the dead center. Slowly deteriorating from all the good things, the good memories I had with Madison. One swift bad move deteriorated all the good I had with her, eating up almost all of it.

~

So, it was the day to put on my fancy suit again I had worn in every Choir concert I attended, to go to Wyatt's prom, my second prom. We went to a local golf center for the nice, fancy prom photos my grandma and Wyatt's Mom shot before us all grabbing a bite to eat and then hitting the dance floor. Photos were my favorite part about prom, to see parents/grandparents snapping them of their grown-up kids all dressed up, about to go to the night of their lives. Not just for Facebook or Instagram, but to also frame them and hang them onto the walls of their houses to show off to parents' friends (which they have the right to do so). To see their little boys and girls once tiny and off to kindergarten now grown into sophisticated young men and women, wishing to freeze time for a day or two.

  The idea of a second prom seemed almost perfect, because own prom was so very much fun, I wanted to relive it all. I love to have a good time.

  The prom was held in an Arts Center, it was exhilarating in the photo booth snapping snapshots with Wyatt. But then he went off with his classmates and I stood on the side of the dance floor - I almost felt alienated and ostracized. I looked around and didn't see a familiar face, unlike at my prom when it was with all my classmates. As I shimmied along to the loud music, smiling as if I was having a great time from the outside, but in the inside, it didn't really feel like my prom. The people and the music surrounding me turned to slow motion and I stopped awkwardly shimming to a complete pause. A pause that was like the world stopped on its axis, stopped orbiting, voices and noises became almost disorienting, almost dream-like, like I was not supposed to be here. Pretty much I had to mask my true feelings similar to a character in a J. D. Salinger novel, the one who thought that everyone surrounding him were morons and phonies. It was a disorienting weird feeling to be at a different class's prom, standing, leaning, sitting on the side like a wallflower, admiring the view and the crowd, like I was in my late thirties watching from afar. Not in a creepy way, but in a way that I was able to look back on my own night of my life, all dressed up in a nice outfit but felt older than my own age.

    I started to wonder 'was this a mistake?' But, no it wasn't a mistake, I had to be there, in the soles of my own fancy shoes. For the record, it was not a mistake, I accepted his invitation to another friend's prom, and I was there for him, but when he disappeared with his friends, in the moment of it all it was like being in the wrong place. In the moment it was all very new, that ostracizing feeling, standing there off to the side, not knowing anyone but Wyatt, in which my neurodiverse brain could look upon that feeling sooner, later that it sunk in. That is another thing I dislike about being an autistic individual, it is almost impossible to be able to detect whatever it is

I'm currently feeling, be in sync, stay in tune to my own emotions. It's also like in the middle of a sensory overload, words failing to express how I felt in those moments. My autism took hold off me. I was there and felt everyone knew I was the autistic individual, not my prom.

*Why is he here?*

It's sad how society ostracized the autism community as 'outlandish' and out of the norm not knowing what to expect from people like us. That night at the second prom I felt excluded in every way at the same time that I was pretending to have fun taking pictures, or going to a photo booth covered with props and making goofy faces while simultaneously the odd feeling of alienation kept growing.

I could only remember that night as 'my second prom' and only that but always remembered my own prom to be the most memorable. Like the sequel to a movie which is never as good as the original. Two proms and that is it. There would not be a third sequel. I was clearly fortunate enough to be able to go to another prom but that was the last. I love dancing, love having a good time, but not with a couple of younger kids who are strangers. Granted they were only one year younger, but in high school that is a big difference.

After all these years were a roller coaster that went up and suddenly came straight down so abruptly yet necessary, as a wake-up call to the newest chapter, the newest road to travel on.

    Like looking at a still-portrait, one side forward, three steps back to see the whole, bigger picture.

    Sometimes memories sneak out of the corners of my eyes and rolls down my cheeks. From all these years from the person I once was to the person I've become, like packing my suitcase to the newest, waving a heartfelt goodbye to the oldest, but cherishing it forever in my mind and heart.

    Those feelings in around May and June hit harder, especially if you're a senior in high school.
    In my case, the fifth year. Goodbyes aren't easy but inevitable, like the tune of a Billie Ellish song. For me, it hit me quite harder than hard because it sunk in that I was officially done with high school.

    In my lifetime, I no longer have to step into a high school to have a good, fun time. There are also other things down the new road that I could be looking forward to.
    Don't know what it is, but I'm more than happy to find out.

## CHAPTER 19 - AFTER ALL THESE YEARS

"Instead, it's one step forward and three steps back / And I'd leave you, but the roller coaster is all I've ever had." ~ Song "1 step forward, 3 steps back" by Olivia Rodrigo

Fellow readers, you made it this far….
The flip of a new chapter, a new breath-of-fresh-air journey awaits me that will feel so new but still prefer my own destiny remains a mystery, without a fortune-teller telling me otherwise.

That was my calling, sometimes it could be disconnected, or discorded, or even unclear, but it's kind of, sort of exciting to remain this way, my own adventures unclear.

That's what makes it more adventurous.

What it felt like an era of the previous era to begin a new chapter.

To flip a new page of that new chapter, instead of rereading the old chapter to seek new, different outcomes and seek out validations from others in order for myself to build up and grow.

To flip to a new chapter of my life, is to seek my own validations for myself by self-loving, to crave for myself, so I don't have to seek it from the world, and for my own free-will.

To flip to a new chapter of my life, into

uncharted waters, breaching different territories that seems so new and exciting and in all terrifying.

After high school, I was assigned to go to a program held at another high school called 'EFRW' and this had me both scared and optimistic for the near-future. It's a program at the High School where young people who had graduated from high school go to this program for a secondary transition for employment in the work field for two years. I found it somewhat kind of strange program in another high school instead of a separate building in which I'll explain at another time.

What I've realized from my adventures down that road, I've paved another cemented road to the future. Of course, as a still young person, I wanted to just focus on summer break and not be in a tizzy about this program to be attended in the fall of 2019. We young people wanted to have fun in the summer instead of being a Rory-F*ing-Gilmore and just enjoy the now-moment than worrying about the roads down ahead.

Going to the beach, being at a Starbucks, creating nice summer vibes, snapping some shots for an Instagram story, reading a nice summer book and going to the movie theaters. The summer times are times to just relax from those years of studying for exams, tests, and everyday attending, walking through the front doors of high school both sometimes in some good, terrific moods to some stressed, not-so-good moods. To just lay low, stress-free, hang out with friends and families in fun summer activities.

Summer times are definitely for young people and adults alike. They are still young enough to still have fun and not always be super serious about every damn thing that requires work or school. We humans, both neurotypicals and neurodiverse, are social butterflies, not operating computer machines as flesh-and-blood with brains, veins and organs. We always overwork ourselves to be successful; there are different definitions in terms of the word and different perceptions of what it really means.

*What is success?*

That could be a rhetorical question or could be answered in your own definitions and perceptions. It's not so black-and-white after all, it is flying colors and not everyone has the same definitions nor idea of what the word 'success' really means and what it stands for.

\*\*\*

After all these years, after all the five years of high school, my life had changed and for the near-future it will continue to change every aspect of me.

As I grow older, my mind is also still

growing, still evolving into a better, a more open version of myself. Growing up is mandatory but evolving is another, separate thing. It ties so beautifully; it's beautifully demystified as I grow up physically as well as mentally and spiritually.

      After all these years traveling that road came to a crossroad, and I was standing in the center, looking north, east, west, and south. How would I know where the heck I should go? I just know. According to Robert Frost, I traveled down the road less traveled and flipped the page to a new breath-of-fresh-air chapter of my life.

## CHAPTER 20: - INTO A NEW CHAPTER

"This Isn't a Hoodie, This Is Adulthood"

Adulthood is like looking both ways before you cross the street and then getting hit by an airplane.

Adulthood is like stepping out of a classroom and then getting sucker-punched the moment you're out of that classroom.

Adulthood is like learning about how to fit into the social norms of society instead of not learning the basic skills we all need in order to thrive in life, like doing taxes.

After all the fun adventures of warm or smoldering hot weather of the summertime, I was anticipating the EFRW program that was to come next and wondered what to expect from this new program I was about to embark on next, to marinate in a new dish of new memories.

Throughout my summer break I googled the website of this program looking for more interesting facts. All I got was the contact list of the teachers and nothing else, not even a link to a possible Twitter (now X) account.

This program was to teach me ways of the world, how to communicate professionally to co-workers and bosses. I was very curious about this program.

*Is it in a separate building?*
*Is it a part of a college?*
*What is this EFRW program?*

The school bus came to pick me up to take me to EFRW and it led to a high school. I thought that was peculiar, thought I was at the wrong place at first, but this was the exact location. I walked toward the red brick building as if I were Meryl Streep in *The Devil Wears Prada*, hiding my true, uncertain feelings brewing inside, not to act like I'm lost, showing no indication that I didn't know where the heck I was going.

It took me a while to find the classroom that holds the EFRW program which made me feel like I was back to square one of my freshman year. Fresh out of middle school, I looked around with lost, beady eyes with the same attitude as if this was middle school still. That was how I walked around the halls of this new high school. It was unclear to me how to find that classroom where the EFRW programs were being held.

Finally, after what it felt like infinity, I found the classroom and it was at the very, very end of the entire high school. I thought that was odd as if it was a secret lair that the students, the staff, or even the facility members hardly knew of. Like an upside-down parallel world beneath the high school.

On the first day we got some interesting

rules, one being that we autistic "interns" were not to interact with the regular High School students. It was well intended but a rule that felt so isolating. Even though most of the young interns such as myself were one year older, others two years older than the regular students, it made us feel that we were much older.

The first few weeks of the EFRW program included morning announcements, activities to learn office etiquette and constant debates on whether to eat lunch at the cafeteria or the classroom. The first few weeks of EFRW was just getting to know how this program worked and to get into the groove of it all, but in such a slow burn fashion that a week felt like months. Most days I would come home with the response 'fine, nothing much' to the question: 'How was your day? What did you do today?' Some of those days felt like a waste of hours. Most of the time we played out office etiquette-based activities, but it was like when I was in high school; I expected so much more, and it felt misleading.

Misleading how you might ask?

In a way that is as if you're expecting a packet in the mail containing a beautiful movie but when that package comes to your front door, it is dish-soap. That's what I more or less felt about this program, because during all my high school days I've heard of this program and it sounded like it would be a new approach to learning, but me sitting at one of the desks in the classroom felt as if I was back to square one.

Yielding to the future, somehow still felt going backward.

***

Finally, after weeks and weeks on end of the same exact things, the teachers of the EFRW program gave us options to go where we wanted to fulfill this training. The choices were to go to a hospital, a country club, or even to be a receptionist at some organization in a strip mall. I chose the receptionist job to expand my clerical knowledge and expertise in that particular field. In my head, it seemed like a pretty decent job, but me sitting on the desk in the front of this little organization in a not-so-safe strip mall was different than I expected. It became a common theme for me, my expectations never met reality.

To be a receptionist there was very much the same thing, every day I sat at the desk waiting for the phone to ring. Other than that, I had little interaction with anyone. The office had one or zero calls a day. The program instructors rarely checked on how I was doing, physically and emotionally. It felt as if they just put me on a boat, pushed me onto the middle of the lake, with no guidance and just a single oar to paddle back to shore, on my own.

My grandma noticed that my socialization skills were slowly deteriorating into a bottomless hole of nothingness. No wonder! I was sitting there at that desk all day by myself, no co-workers in sight, no teachers to check on me, and the phone rang once a day.

One day, when I was again sitting at the receptionist desk for yet another torturous 8-hour day, I heard someone from outside of the complex screaming, yelling profanity. I thought that was peculiar and strange and I shrugged my shoulders like it was nothing, like 'yeah, somebody woke up on the wrong side of the bed' and didn't think more of it. Until this woman walked into the reception area where I was sitting with this sad, desperate look on her face that indicated that she needed help, like right now. Of course, with my generosity, I had to try to help this profanity spewing, desperate woman. I wouldn't be that one person to make it much worse than it already was for her by throwing the trump card that I'm 'an intern'. I said, "How can I help?" My weeks-long office etiquette training was finally paying off. And she talked frantically about some financial issues and challenges, and I just nodded. After going on for a few more minutes and me just nodding she calmed down – like all neurotypical people, she sniffed out my neurodiversity within minutes – and realizing I could not meet her needs she showed some gratitude "Thank you for trying," she said, calmer, but left in despair, her face distorted with stress.

Little did I know that outside my own world, my own universe, peering out the window from it all was a totally different world. This woman from outside my building, who shouted out profanity was the kind of person who was struggling financially or just generally woke up to a$$holes who refused to show little care and help her. It was somewhat an epiphany, a small epiphany that gently shook my world. Being a receptionist in this office I got a front row seat to someone else's life – that there is more to it than meets the eyes, lives aren't black-and-white.

Another anxiety crept up when I was sitting at the receptionist desk. What if the same kind of person as the woman who shouts out profanity comes into my lobby feeling a fiery hatred about to boil over. I would blame the EFRW teachers for not preparing me for helping people like that desperate woman. Luckily, she calmed down after getting to know me, realizing she was screaming at the wrong person, but the anxiety came to me like 'what if someone like her came to me but more fiery, angry stepped inside'. My reason for blaming the teachers is what I said earlier where they metaphorically put me on a boat in the middle of a lake, with no to little guidance, just an oar to paddle back to shore.

I didn't tell the teachers about my experiences with the yelling woman and me trying to help her and never told them how I truly felt about being in that little building, at the receptionist desk, being in my own head all day long until a disgruntled customer showed up. But I did tell my grandma and she wanted to call the school, but I begged her not to, after all wasn't the point of EFRW to prepare me for the real world when I couldn't run to my grandma, aunt or mom for every little issue I had.

## CHAPTER 21 - MY CHOICE - TO DISCLOSE OR NOT TO DISCLOSE

…that is the question.

This is no Hamlet, but this is a revelation about this whole thing.

Something that I learned as a rude awakening, and that was the choice to disclose my own autism when I opened myself for a position at a job.

In my mind, I thought about disclosing my own intellectual disability to the workforce, worrying about how others would think of me. Thinking I'm just using it as a free pass?

This chapter in the next page will discuss it further in depth in how I feel about it and it may sound distasteful and seems like I'm attacking the autism community.

Hey, what I gotta do, what I gotta do. I think the autism community needs a little brutally honest speakers in order to get autism representations and to be taken seriously.

The choice to disclose or not to disclose my autism when I stepped out into the workforce was a question I couldn't immediately answer. Do I on the first day of an interview say, "I have autism?" *Or should I just be myself and let them figure out what was going on?* To open up my autism for both the employees and employers in any given occupation I would be able to get immediate accommodations. I opposed the idea though, to be treated differently because of that, to disclose, to open up, telling them about my own disadvantages, putting my condition on display for the employees and employers to see.

It should be my choice to disclose my autism, opening up, dissecting parts by parts, or keeping it to myself until the time is absolutely right for me, until I feel comfortable to talk to someone about it. Not some stranger sitting in an office.

Even before setting foot into this program, even before learning about this program when I was in the five years of high school, I didn't expect to hear:

*Oh, hey, ugh, when you step into this program you need to disclose your autism.*

*Does everyone have to disclose their shortcomings? Hey, I have anxiety? I have high cholesterol? What about some privacy, please?*

It was blunt and unexpected, almost like being sucker punched that the EFRW program gave me the *opportunity*" to disclose.

The fear of me disclosing my own autism is also about how the employees will handle that private information their bosses tell them: one of the interns or the new co-worker happens to have autism. *Would they think that I only disclosed it to use it as a free pass to accommodate me and not wanting to equally work along with the employees as if I wasn't autistic? Would I be bullied for disclosing it as if I couldn't handle the effects of real life and reality?*

    I know the program had good intentions for me to have the option to disclose my own autism, so the employer would have a piece of an understanding about me as an autistic, neuro-diverse person, but deep down in my core I don't think disclosing it was the slightest, perfect option to choose from. For instance, I can choose to accommodate my needs without making my autism a big deal, like I would say something like 'Hey I'm Lewis and I can do anything I can try to muster," thus not putting my autism on display, on a pedestal. I do know that some people have it worse than me, that they have to tell their bosses and some of their co-workers about their autism in order to get the help and accommodations they need. Yes, I have autism, but I don't always want to put it on a name tag. I know the fact that I cannot change who the F I am and just accept the fact that I have autism, but it is just the fear of disapproval once they spread the news; as if I was a sea monster, disguised, hiding in my human form. Even though over and over again I've been accepting myself for being the way I am, I still don't grasp the fact that I would potentially be ostracized by someone just for being myself and have to remind myself that it won't just take overnight to make it all go away. I don't want it to go away, it is who I am, but deep down I could feel the fear of being ostracized, just because I can't do it."

In the classroom of EFRW while we were talking about the options of disclosing my autism, I sat there, quiet and uncomfortable. Again, I was that person, sitting down quietly and not amplifying my voice through a megaphone, which is my strength of a good rebellion. If you don't like something, the options are to voice it loudly and passionately, or you could take a different route to be silent yet uncomfortable and oppose it with an *unbelievable* scoff.

Mr. Thompson noticed the look on my face. "What?" He wanted to know more. I shrugged. I couldn't put into words exactly how I felt and also didn't feel like pouring out all my thoughts to him. The teachers in the program were often indifferent, and Mr. Thompson who was older than the rest of the other teachers, was a cranky older man whose mind was so closed, it was locked shut with scatters of rusts. We would usually do morning announcements and watch a few minutes of CNN-10 to learn what's going on outside of the borders of our worlds. We would discuss what we just watched and when one of us, the interns, disagreed or weren't paying attention, Mr. Thompson would chime in with so much arrogance that we are too focused on our phones versus this discussion we were having, and not understand, but that he wouldn't expect any better from our generation.

He was one of those people who refused to see a whole new possibility of the immense opportunity of teaching the next generations to take on the world. He often loved to argue with the other teachers, as well as argue with one of us. Sometimes, I wondered why Mr. Thompson was even teaching; ranting about everything, *was he that miserable at home, or about his age? What made him so?* I could not figure it out. He would at times rant about the fact that we were autistic, or young and arrogant, always on our phones, having headphones on, always having this repressed look of not giving a sh*t about our own futures.

You know, the stigma of the generation gap, constant budding heads between the old and the young and continuous recessive looks from the old man as if he viewed the young as a disgusting disgrace, the downfall of society.

While Mr. Thompson was yammering on and on, ranting on and on about how much of a disgrace and a disappointment he felt we were, it occurred to me that he maybe just wanted to break us down to build us up. A rude awakening from walking through life so blindly, so sleepily that also ignited what I've already known, to be a quiet rebel, not the kind that shouts through a megaphone.

You may ask, what am I rebelling for? Like,

rebelling in a way to voice my own voice in how hypocritical Mr. Thompson was ranting on and on about our generation. He ranted on about us listening to music or being on the phones – we should instead focus on him, but it was just the way he blew a fuse that shut me down.

He would do a five, seven minutes long rant and then when that absurd rant was over, he would just whip out his iPhone as if the rant didn't mean a thing. It was like when the pot calls the kettle black, guilty of the same thing: he looked at his phone.

For instance, we were remembering 9/11 and Mr. Thompson would shake his head as if he was the only person living on this earth who had more experiences than us. He explained that most of us, my generation, born in the late, or the mid- 1990s and beginning of the 2000s were still babies or very young toddlers when the two planes were hijacked and crashed into the World Trade Center, when the other two, one attempted to crash into the White House but instead crashed on a field in Pennsylvania and the other crashed into the Pentagon.

Yes, most of us were very, very young and we were talking about 9/11 as if we were there that day, but of course we weren't, because yes, we were small, care-free children at some daycare or home . But we weren't the same innocent children as we grew into our early twenties. We live in the aftermath of that day and grew sentimental because some of those kids had families who worked at the Pentagon and at the World Trade Center. Even though those kids were clueless then of the surrounding world, over time their families would have to break the news to them about parents who did not make it, and the kids would have to live with that for the rest of their lives.

"You are lucky you're not one of those kids. I know a few who went through this." Mr. Thompson ranted. As if it was our fault that our families got away unharmed.

That whole thing of when Mr. Thompson was ranting over the fact that we were so young when that day happened and how lucky we were, I wanted to just say something but didn't because of the fear of being chewed out. That's when I knew this program wasn't for me at all. This wasn't preparing us for the real world. Ranting on about how we have it so good, how we don't have respect for the older generation, I just sat there shaking my head and scoffed silently. And whenever Mr. Thompson or any teacher asked what the scoff was about, I always just shrugged. How could I ever convince them that I'm not that person they labeled me as?

Yes, we all should have respect for one another, including the teachers. But Mr. Thompson forgets that respect is a double-edged sword, for him it goes one way - we should respect him but not the other way - he doesn't respect me or us. Respect has to be earned. He never earned my respect.

One intern asked about dressing up for Halloween and one of the other teachers replied, "You are in your early twenties!" He thought we are adults and cannot have fun, but I still have to have fun because life is still a long, windy road from the start to finish and it all can't always be rushed and serious. Any of this program's good intentions were overwritten with the bad, because there were a few teachers who had little passion but were brutally honest. It's good to be brutally honest and to toughen us up, to prepare us for what life throws at you, but they were so brutally honest that they thought they could outlaw Halloween, not allowing us to celebrate by dressing in costumes. They thought they needed to take away our innocence or any fun in order to be adults. I realize teachers in different counties in America are being overworked and often paid minimum wages. Some teachers are fully committed to helping the kids of the future learn and have passion, providing encouragement and enlightenment. They are committed to teaching the kids of the future, realizing their hard work will pay off when those kids grow up to take on the world to possibly be the next President of the United States of America or the next astronaut. But that was not the case in this program. And there are people that'll enter my life that will either build me up stronger or bring me down, tied up to an anchor to drag me down to the bottom of the ocean. Mostly this EFRW program was bringing me down, made me into an adult by ripping out my own innocence to achieve that. What I mean about that, the teachers tried to take away something that meant so much to me, was deeply burrowed inside of me that I wasn't like a piece of cake to be dismantled, right then and there.

    I rebelled by wearing my cool leather jacket, disguising it as 'normal clothes' but really, it's a costume from a '60s movie in which the lead actor James Dean wore leather jackets. That was my prime example of rebellion to wear "costumes" disguised as normal clothes, as cloaks, to have a double meaning, by slightly tricking them right under their noses. To give out, to convey that I'm still young and that life is a long stretch besides the saying 'grow up!'

    Life is short and we have to cherish every moment of it and not rush it, is my mantra. As a kid, like so many kids in the world, I day-dreamed about being an adult, day-dreamed about the things I wanted to do when I got to that point; like eat lots of junk foods and staying up late. But the moment I reached the age of 19 to 20 years old, the programs tried so hard to forcefully make us want to grow up in the harshest way – we can't dress up for Halloween or can't have fun - in order to endure the real world and the responsibility of it.

    That was my rude awakening, my epiphany

about the real world and about reality. That I have to enjoy while I can, cherish every given moment in the present times with a great mass of gratitude. It's as if I were in Walt Disney World in that one line on the bridge of an Elton John song, feeling like a little kid, indeed. There's no need to be a Peter Pan, to prohibit the idea of growing up; no not that restrictive, but there has to be some advantages to a happy medium.

    I wanted to live life to the fullest, and I'm adding my own spin on it, with a great deal of mass gratitude and enjoy being young as long as possible. It's not just given or taken.

    I do have this drive to thrive where the keys in my brain have been turned, the ignition and the motors of my mind have been activated and I would be zooming across a straight, long country road.

    You may be puzzled, may be a bit confused at this moment, at this point, scratching your head as if you're reading *The Goldfinch*, like 'where the heck is this going?'

    Well, let me tell you the rest.

    Think of it like this: it's seven in the morning, you just brewed some coffee, poured creamer into your cup and then, the coffee itself. Then, take one sip of it and the motors have been activated to start the day. You might've thought, 'wait a burger-flippin' minute? You drink coffee?' Well, for a matter-the-fact, I do. Just because I have a neurodivergent brain, I sure do drink it as if I hadn't. Coffee is my gasoline; it gives me energy to start the day, and I would have leftover energy from the coffee as a drive to thrive even when I was in the EFRW program. It does give me strength, but I'm not just dependent on it, my drive to thrive isn't just dependent on caffeine. There's something within me, almost like a spark, a little fire burning, blazing inside me, doing the things I could and can while it is slowly burning, not to a crisp, but to a sizzle. It has been this way since I stepped into the very first years of high school, that spark, that little fire inside me that wasn't just a teenage angst but gave my life a purpose for my own wellbeing.

That was my drive to thrive then.

Still is now.

That eternal flame inside me, the stored caffeine, wasn't an angst. I wasn't angry, I was just a little ball of energy that just wanted to find the meaning and purpose of what I was feeling that gave me, again, life. It is as if I were Avatar Korra when she was being poisoned with mercury and was able to fight it off. Everybody has their own purpose, both neurotypicals and neurodivergent alike. We are all the same human beings, just with different ways of thinking and in different mindsets that'll make us unique and add pops of bright colors, so it isn't so black-and-white. That is also why I even have the eternal flame within me because while it is burning, sizzling, it is my way of living, my ways of motivation and to be motivated. A goal placed in mind, the eternal flame has been ignited, and the small piece of the flame shown in my irises and my pupils.

You're probably wondering how this flame started in the first place. Well, I can tell you . . . maybe because other people in my past were telling me the things I can or can't do. It is like in the spring of 1887 when a two-term President, Grover Cleveland, who met with a young Franklin D. Roosevelt and had a strange wish upon the young Roosevelt. That strange wish was, in his words, and that was "My little man, I'm making a strange wish for you. It's that you may never be president of the United States" to the young boy that he may never, ever be the future president of that same country. But, forty-eight years later in 1933, a whole new decade emerged, the country was deteriorating from the Great Depression and the brown, circling dust. Yet came a man in a tailored suit who was later in a wheelchair, the same boy who Cleveland wished upon that he shall never be president, yet he became the thirty-second US President.

When I first heard this story, I was elated with joy, knowing I'm not alone in wanting to expand my own territories into trying something out of my comfort zone, even if people tell me I can't; believing that I can do it, and somehow discard when any person thinks that I cannot do it. I was never really alone, because some of those powerful men and women of the past also dealt with the same as I and it is refreshing to ever realize that I'm never, ever really alone, and don't need to wallow in my self-pity. It's important to research and understand the past of those individuals that came before me and also had to deal with the same sliver of issues within themselves as I.

'Great minds all think alike' as they say.

For instance, any powerful figure of the past is flawed and has some rust lingering in the cracks of their nice, shiny armor. Almost like a picture-perfect portrait, so neat, so polished that a precise, perfectionist painter could paint something so gleamingly glossy and so smooth that it almost looked life-like in a way. Almost like reading up a powerful figure's success story but discarding the setbacks and the bad and the ugly and the failures along with his or her success story.

When a person pulls a wish like Grover Cleveland did to Franklin D. Roosevelt to someone who doesn't seem capable of anything, it's almost like putting an idea in their heads, putting the odds in their heads not to break their spirits but to act against. Like going against a rough current of a raging river.

I sure do love reading about those stories because it proves that every person that ever walked on earth who ever dealt with others who broke them down was able to build themselves back up again; or just to make assumptions about a person thinking "he or she only ought to do this or that," thinking about their limits. I say, to me, life is limitless.

As the former First Lady Roosevelt said, "never let anybody make you feel inferior, without your consent." Utilize the odds to something great of your own potential. Don't think of it as a heavy brick being thrown at you and don't let that negativity bring you down. You just got to know what the limits are instead of blandly, bleakly accepting it all as if it's true. In some ways there are limits but in other areas there are not.

That is my drive to thrive.

Out of all the not-so-good experiences during the EFRW program, a decision slowly sizzled within me. My slow-burn dislike started to grow about this program, and I came up with a solution. I was more eager than ever to chase after a potential Full High School Diploma and start a semester at a community college.

So it begins, and oh, it's on!

## CHAPTER 22 - A SMALL CHANGE THAT LED TO SOMETHING BIG

In EFRW there was also Ms. Crombstone; she was in her fifties and when I walked behind her, I couldn't help but notice how much her back swung back and forth. Just like Mr. Thompson she often would rant and rant about how we young people don't even slightly care about our own future, how music and video games were more important, but she forgets, deep down, burrowed in the deep, deep soil of our young souls we do care. Over and over again, she and Mr. Thompson and others, every morning showed nothing but resentment, scuffing, and snarling at us for our own individualities. They had given up on us long before they even got to know us. They made us to be ashamed of who we are.

Teachers like Mr. Tompson and Ms. Crombstone continued to change my perception about the whole program, almost like in the Hulu show, The Handmaid's Tale, where women dressed in red robes and white bonnets that interfered with their peripheral visions. That comparison gave me both confidence and fear that all the good intentions were overwritten, taking over, making people like me think that we 'were not in the papers. We lived in the blank white spaces at the edges of print . . . We lived in the gaps between the stories.' In both the show and the book, the women have to bear children for different families.

None of the teachers came to the job sites to check in on us to see how we were doing both mentally and physically. I really felt like I was on a boat and the EFRW teachers just pushed me from the shores, and I had no or little guidance and an oar to paddle myself back to shore.

I'm a neurodivergent person and always will be but I was a young adult, and they still needed to give me instructions.

The teachers also didn't update our parents, thinking we are adults and could handle ourselves fine, but in a program like this the teachers should update the parents because the parents, or guardians have a right to know about what their kids are doing. Both my grandma and my aunt would find themselves in debates with them about how they should know what and where I'm going and what I'm doing. Maybe they didn't want my family to know that at times I was working in a hotel changing sheets and scrubbing toilets.

My grandmother and my aunt wouldn't just coddle me, wrap a cozy blanket around me like I'm Baby Yoda sipping a bowl of soup with glee and comfort. They hardened, toughened me up with words because they knew what was expected of me and I sure as heck knew that too. Despite my autism, I only would be my limits. It's a good thing to have people in my life, in my family, in my blood, to toughen me rather than soften me from the facade, because they sure do care for me and I'm forever grateful about that.

It's such a wonder, a beauty, to have people in my family that made me who I'm today and for the future, teaching me what to expect in and from life as a whole. They just wanted the best and did the best from the well-being of me. Not trying to be the smartest in the room, they just genuinely want me to be the best in my own abilities regarding my own limits that makes me limitless.

With all this amount of dislikes about this particular program, I gave myself little choice, but to chase after the possibility of a full High School Diploma by completing that one final SOL test in order to masterfully achieve and receive it, because the program has an expired age date; at the age of twenty-one, I wouldn't be eligible for the program and I was twenty at the time but I didn't want to spend another year and half at this program.

I needed my high school diploma, so I could be done.

Of course, the common theme of the story of my life is the teachers tossing the trump card of what I 'can't do,' or 'this is way over your head.' Yes, the "Reading" SOL was my kryptonite, but I knew one day I would pass it. My grandma got me lots of SOL reading material and my aunt practiced with me, but it all was very hard. I don't know why it is that some teachers use their willpower to only break me down, telling me the opposite of what my family was saying rather than the equivalents.

"You can do this," my aunt and grandma and mom said.

"It's too much for you," the teachers said.

Groups of people look and frown upon the people who appear to be different and abnormal; always assume that people like me couldn't do the same sh*t as someone who doesn't have the same thing as me.

"It's the easy way out," my grandma says. It's easier to give up on someone than to work hard with someone to get there. So, I continued to chase after that full High School Diploma and my family instilled the fuel and the willpower and the stubbornness to go after it. All my hate and dislike about the EFRW program gave me even more energy towards achieving and receiving that F*ing diploma. Oh, so, you expect a neurodivergent person like me to never spew out profanity with some force and integrity? You expect a neurodivergent person such as myself to ever just be the sweetest, soft, kind, gentle soul that never a sliver of bad profanity would slip out my mouth? There are no rulebooks to using bad, naughty language; there is a difference from being a jerk or just using that to prove my point.

Many neurodivergent voices on the spectrum and in the community are people who are fighting, striving, thriving - in all, we are all different yet the same, just different definitions of success. I sure as heck know that there's going to be a long road of discovery, even after the end of adolescence, into adulthood.

*Why at the end of adolescence, the coming-of-age, do I have to have things all figured out entirely and immediately be ready for this new age of adulthood? Why is there always a program that only focuses on the facade but not the insides?* A program to have the good intentions to teach people like us the ways of the world, the ways of the cold, cruel world that high school doesn't teach the slightest?

I even had daydreams of myself being the Governor of Virginia, dismantling the EFRW program and having imaginary arguments with the EFRW teachers about that, because there is something more than meets the eyes, more than just the pretty facades. Less focusing on the outside garden, but more focusing on the things inside before you.

Yes, it is good to prepare people like me for ways of the world, but no, it is not good to have underpaid, mentally unwell, unpassionate people running those programs only focusing on the outside, less on the inside; almost like to show, to talk about the successes but cancel out the failures. The two need to be interwoven into one, become one, in order to tell it in the most poignant way.

Small changes could lead to something big, to make an impact on yourself and others surrounding me. For the greater good. Often misunderstood in what I really want to convey to others, afraid of how others perceive me. *Perceive me how?* In a way I'm so driven, so confident, but yet still so insecure that it is such a burden weighing a thousand tons over my shoulders. The kind of burden where everybody totally discards that Walt Whitman quote rather than being on a high horse, looking down, frowning upon others as if they don't F*ing understand, like they are still in the twentieth century. Over time repressing myself, my own needs, and my own emotions for just a long time that'll take more, more and more time to retrain my brain into reconsidering. For these reasons, I just keep telling myself as if I'm looking at an apparition of myself, arguing with myself about why I repress myself.

It may seem unclear but one thing that sticks out from my repressions is that I just want and need to please everyone and need to make my own presence scream that. Putting my own needs aside to help others, that's the kind of person I am, as if I were in an airplane having to place an oxygen mask on the person next to me rather than my own. The other thing is that, for me, saying 'no' sounds like an insult or me not trying hard enough. Also, me saying 'no' makes me perceive that I'm just a lazy person who someone frowns upon prior to me saying it.

That word is my frenemy, it's both beneficial and problematic. Also, I've said that no matter how much, how hard I try, I could still be insecure trying to match others' levels of perceptions. I don't need to not be neurotypical, as if my values don't have values at all. I feel the same feeling as any human being on this beloved earth, just can't convey and distinguish those feelings as if that would be so easy, like a piece of cake.

It's not meant to be easy.

Small changes that lead to something big, to wake up from sleepwalking through life.

Small changes that lead to something big, to reconsider myself as a person, not an entity without emotions or feelings.

Small changes that lead to something big, to be able to say 'no' and not to toss my own needs aside to help others. I just need to know what my limits are and not jump immediately if or when I'm not in the right mindset to do so.

Small changes that lead to something big, to normalize the feeling of being insecure, to not view that as a stigma and only view it as part of human growth.

Yes, I'm driven. I carry myself as a unique individual. But I could just normalize the fact that it is and will be OK to have those unpleasant feelings, not to only corrupt my own happiness but to also look at that as growth. Just because I have a neurodiverse brain but try to act as if I don't have one, I think like any other human being on the planet, just don't know how to convey those feelings or express myself as well as some do.

At EFRW, when I mentioned I would want to work at Starbucks, the teacher said it's too high paced, again someone telling me I can't do something.

"Be curious, not judgmental. ~ Walt Whitman."

What often holds me back from doing the things I want in life is the fear of rejections or the fear of resentment from others' perceptions and assuming something about me before even getting to know me. Neurodiverse or not, holding back and not advocating for myself is my worst kryptonite, robbing me of slivers of happiness.

But what people don't realize is that they do have the power to break down my spirits, piece by piece, brick by brick, but I will rebuild the torn-up, shattered remains of myself and reconstruct myself.

How awkward would it be for those same people who managed to successfully break my spirits, break me down as a whole, and then come to find a newly refurbished version of myself, looking at me face-to-face? I would have to thank them with glee and grace. Thanking them for tearing down the previous foundations of my own well-being, that there were slight hints of good intentions. Sure, in the beginning, it was like being betrayed, for being winded after a tremendous blow to the stomach. Heck, you could sucker punch, or even sucker spit me, and I will thank you with glee. Yes, at the moment, I would be like 'hey, what the heck' but, at the end of the day, thanking you. Anything post-that, in the beginning, unpleasant feelings of resentment, anger, and possibly the feelings of being like a hexagon peg in a circle-shaped hole are inevitable. Overtime, it molded and grew on me and the realization kicked in and then, the gratitude as well.

  Overall, I'm a nice person, not trying to give into some person's bad intentions to intercept it with the good. I only justified the results in the end to better understand it. Deep down I just knew what was better for my own future and what my future self could look back on, glance at and chuckle about it.

## CHAPTER 23 - 2020: A ZOOM ODYSSEY

Something my past self would have never thought of; something so life-changing that my entire livelihood changes along with it. Almost like a square peg trying to fit into a circle hole, to endure, to deal with new growing pain that even a neurodivergent person doesn't know how to deal with.

Cue the "2001: A Space Odyssey" theme, because that would be an out-of-this-world, bumpy jump into the hyperspace wild thrill ride.

During my super-senior year, I recall somewhere in November, or December 2019 hearing briefly of a new virus forming in Wuhan, China (a city I had never heard of back then) but didn't pay much attention, because I figured it would be sorted out like all the other viruses we have dealt with in the past: specialists in those areas would keep this newly formed, newly developed virus at bay like they did with the Ebola or swine flu viruses, for example.

Burrowing deep down like a rabbit, it was pretty bad, so bad that my 2019-self and my 2021-self came together to discuss one another at a local coffee place someplace.

My 2019-self would've never thought that my 2021-self would be wearing a hundred-percent cotton mask, intensely rubbing hand sanitizer on my hands after touching just anything and getting very jarringly skittish when hearing a nearby sneeze or cough. Probably my 2019-self would have cocked his head like *what is the big deal?* when first hearing about this virus. Also, my 2019-self would not have thought that the final SOL test I had to pass, might not be required in order to receive that full high school diploma, but my 2021-self would never leak that kind of information to my past self, because my past dictates itself.

    So, my 2021-self just kept his mouth shut and nodded to what my past self was worrying about - SOLs. Only the hundred-percent cotton mask or an N-95 mask, and the hand sanitizer spoke for themselves, they did all the talking. Those were the vessel to my 2021 self's shield and armor of this growing pandemic and my past self would have never thought of those things.

    That saying in every sci-fi movie, 'I'm you, in the future' and if I imagined my past 2019-self and 2021-self sitting face-to-face at a coffee shop it would feel like a *Black Mirror* episode that reality certainly felt surreal. My 2021 self, wearing the mask, barely speaking, but the mask was doing the talking; communicating telepathically with my eyes. "Help!" they screamed.

    My 2021-self telepathically speaking to my young self, 'You would have not thought that your near-future self, sitting across from you, wearing this hundred-percent cotton mask, constantly worrying if other people would follow the six feet distance rule.'

And my young 2019-self would just look, glare at my current self as if I had gone mad and not saying anything back. Only glare.

"Who would've thought I'd be trapped in my house, wearing masks when going anywhere at all, and having to keep a safe distance from others?"

It all changed the way I interacted with people, by no longer going to a movie theater or the mall, nor Starbucks to order a drink I could post on social media.

When I first heard of this virus forming in China it didn't really occur to my mind that one, little virus could change everything. I just wished it to be contained and to be gone within days.

Initially, I was cool, calm and collected about the whole thing, keeping an optimistic viewpoint, that "they" would contain it. Not exactly sure who "they" were, but I figured it will resolve itself. This is how I was and still how I'm today, looking at the positive side of things.

Me sitting in the EFRW classroom, watching the morning news of CNN-10 during which the reporters were talking about this virus in Wuhan, two things happened in my mind. (1) The optimistic feeling that this virus could be happily contained and (2) The worries snuck through; a tiny ounce within me said that this is not like the other viruses. I had my 'oh god' moment inside, but still filtered it with everlasting optimism and hope that this virus would be carefully contained and controlled.

~

In the beginning of March 2020 there were oblivious people everywhere, some didn't even know it was happening; as if this was an M. Night Shyamalan movie.

I remember both my grandmother and my aunt fighting their battles with the EFRW program teachers to pull me out of that classroom to safety from this invisible, airborne outbreak. My grandma watched what was happening in Europe and saw the writing on the wall. Some didn't or couldn't believe it was happening; some literally thought my grandma and aunt were overreacting pulling me out of the program.

My teacher wrote an email to my grandma: "I implore you to keep Lewis in this program…"

I'm forever grateful that both my aunt and my grandmother stuck their arms out to pull me into safety. I no longer needed to go my new job site, which meant I no longer needed to clean toilets at a hotel.

Three weeks later everything shut down. March 2020 when WHO (WHO?! Who's WHO?! Oh, the World Health Organization) declared a pandemic and we had to stay home and to stay safe and to replace all our humanly, daily routines from walking to Starbucks, to a mall, or to a restaurant, or even to the movie theaters, replaced them with Zoom and watch new movies that were released to Disney Plus, HBO Max and other streaming services in the comfort of our home.

Something that my newly minted January 2020 self would have never thought that in the span of three months we'd be kept in the house from an invisible, air-borne virus. Would have not thought of wearing masks and keeping six feet of distance from others, loose acquaintances, friends, and even family members.

Would have not thought of the things we love most, and we do on a daily basis, taken for granted, would come to an abrupt halt to be replaced by online interactions like Zoom.

It all took a different direction in terms of a virus that changed and rocked my, along with other people's worlds. Who would have thought from New Year's Day 2020 to just a few months down the slightly rocky to an even rockier road of Spring of 2020?

Changed in the ways we used to do things we took for granted.

It was a surreal time in the very beginning of it all, something that I could tell my future kids about. Surreal and weird how it all started.

My parents had planned a cruise that was supposed to take place in April, and they even got me a brand-new, light-blue suitcase and I was so looking forward to the trip.

All the plans had to be just flat-out canceled, like a show after one season.

The virus rose like a fierce phoenix out of the ashes, and it was frighteningly scary and being pulled out of the program was the best thing ever. Others would think my family and I were going crazy, yet we were making rational decisions for the long run.

It was so hard for the EFRW teachers to wrap their heads around how to continue the program online. None of us ever thought about how to continue something on Zoom for which you actually had to be there in person. It was like sailing onto newly uncharted waters for which no maps had been charted yet.

\*\*\*

At the start of April 2020, it was a very new thing for me to continue the EFRW program online, on Zoom. I don't really remember much of what I've learned, but we watched a lot of news together and discussed it.

Towards the end of the school year our state Governor waived the SOL testing for all Virginia

High School students – I couldn't believe it. I had that one final SOL left in reading, my kryptonite, and now the Governor was saying don't worry about it. It clearly was my golden ticket to that coveted full High School Diploma I had been striving for all my high school years.

However, my EFRW teachers weren't sure if waiving the SOLs would apply to us super-seniors.

My grandma didn't understand their reluctance. Why would it be any different for me? The Governor said, "all high school students."

We waited a bit longer since the teachers were debating, "should we treat the neurodiverse differently? Do they fall under the same rules? Did the Governor include them?" The EFRW administrator put the question out there and still we had to wait.

*Does he deserve that diploma?*

It was exhausting. All the teachers I've encountered in the high school that were…., I don't know, but they were just miserable or just wanted to teach the kids including myself about life of how F*ing miserable it is. That it is not all walking on sunshine and finding the ends of rainbows and riding on magical, ridiculously pink and purple unicorns.

Even before this virus struck, I was assigned a course in the high school where the teachers I've met were just miserable yet said they had good intentions for me to be successful in life, but the performance and deliverances, a roller coaster straight down, my friend. Overall, I'm a nice person, but I got tired of the teachers in that EFRW program doing everything possible to treat us differently. The good intentions were there, but the bad was overwritten as if this were a video game. And I thought, 'Gosh! I wished I could just snatch that diploma and just run with it.' I hated the whole experience of being in that high school where it did affect my entire mood; it was a gray, quiet, miserable, overcast version of it: it was purgatory.

After weeks of a tug-of-war, asking "do we waive the SOL for the neurodiverse, also, or only the neurotypical," I finally received the biggest news: My SOL would also be waved; it was decided, the super-seniors would be treated the same.

I finally would get my full high school diploma!

I could not believe it. I would finally be a high school graduate!

It was a huge milestone in my life, the silver lining of the pandemic, me holding it up in the air like I'm in the Special Olympics or something, or the ending scene of the movie *The Breakfast Club*.

I achieved my full High School Diploma! It was the recycled feeling of when I walked with my peers in a navy-blue robe-like Superman in a cape! I felt empowered and fantastic all over again and received that diploma with me running straight to the finish line and never looking back. I received that thing, now have it in my hands and will not look back to the EFRW program.

The program made me a different person from when I first stepped into the classroom, when I was so lost. It changed me from the naïve high school senior to the super senior, to freshly see the world differently. I metaphorically took off the old, crusty pink eye-contacts and replaced them with a new one of real life.

As much as I hated the program, it also molded me into a new person and made me who I became today. I'm more realistic, less of a dreamer. I see how much people have to work in hotels, cleaning, or how hard it is sitting at a desk job all day which will suck out any and all of your spirits. Despite my autism, I'm driven and carry myself differently than the rest, because autism is a span of different types of people, not just one group. I still have that drive ever since, and you may ask 'where the heck did that come from?' and I would simply answer 'well, I don't know,' shrug and shake my head. Maybe because my family always pushing me and expecting more?

"Don't let being autistic define you," they said. But, it's OK not to know how that drive inside me continues to thrive in me. On the spectrum, even we are labeled the same, but depending on the 'ables' that makes us uniquely different from the rest, even within the spectrum.

I finally had my full high school diploma, and I dreaded the next few remaining weeks of the Zoom-version of the program until the beginning of Summer when I finally would be done. But I made it and during a full-fledged pandemic, I was entirely and finally done with Highschool and being a super senior in the EFRW program.

I decided to go to a community college in the fall.

Therefore, out of all the gray, miserable parts encountered, a positive ray of sunshine molted from negativity to positivity. It made me a new kind of person that wouldn't take no bullsh*t from others who would think less of me.

Being a super senior taught me also a dark side of those programs for people with autism that need help to be successful in the real world, to fit in the status quo but we were told we would have to adjust in order to fit in. The Caregivers of Autism told me that people in society are going to be mean and it'll be harder if I don't fit the status quo without accommodations, that people with autism are just have to suck it the F up and deal with it, try to be like others, because that is "life." Yes, we autistic people have autism Yes, we are born with it (or something happened during birth?). Yes, we were diagnosed with it and no, to the people who just want to ignore or get rid of autism without even learning anything about autism, I can't change them. Yes, we are different from neurotypicals, yes, we think absolutely different. Yes, we want and like things in a certain way, but no, we aren't using autism as a name-tag to breeze through life. I've been telling myself to learn what my limits are and that means to not quit so easily and to just try and if I fail, that's OK.

Again, those kind of programs do have good intentions and good representations among autistic people to learn to fit into the world and into society. And that is OK to accommodate us, in order to fit into it. Some of us can read, some of us can't, it's just how our brains and minds work. Our wants, desires, and needs are generally the same as somebody who is a neurotypical, we just have different approaches in how we communicate and how that is perceived. Communication isn't our strong suit, isn't our strength, but there would be no excuses to not take us seriously.

Autism is put on pedestals for awareness for others to learn what it is to be autistic, and now to shine brightly of blue and we are showered with puzzle-piece-infused ribbons that no longer represent us autistic people. I know the intentions are good - to shine a light on the representations of autism, but just changing the bulbs to blue could also trigger a sensory overload.

I can totally see why it's hard on both sides:

the one side of caregiving autistic people, accommodating for a comfortable, happy life and the other, the autistic people and the way their brains and minds work, like constantly climbing a wall to get to the other side. Everything is a constant effort to be autistic, but that is just the disadvantage. Autism is more than repetitive behaviors; constantly repeating themselves and needing things done a certain way. I'm also autistic, not a person with autism, I don't carry it in a plastic Target bag. It's a part of me, not a part of me. I can't distinguish. I can't separate my own autism from my own self, because without my autism, I'll be a totally different human being. And this constant theme wraps around my brain that I'm a human being with feelings, with rights, and with values and morals, yet one more characteristic: autistic. Somehow, I forget I have rights, that I have feelings, and that I also have values just as somebody who doesn't have autism. I always keep forgetting I have those things, as if in the back of my head, a voice keeps telling me the opposite and I do always listen to that. Like a parasite.

  Burrow deep like a sand flea; I know who the F I am.

  With that full High School diploma in my grasp and me traveling down a whole new, the road less traveled and the feel of breaking into song as if I'm in a damn musical, good god.

  I got the diploma; I reached the milestone.

Milestone' Something to look upon, something to reach, that is a major thing to get by.

Some people just like to assume someone who is diagnosed with autism, or any kind of learning disabilities will not have a happy, everlasting life to ever be satisfied.

That it could be a burden to some,

That it could be a blessing to another.

That there could be others who just won't don't understand.

With my diploma in hand, I still had to deal with the pandemic. Being kept inside was so surreal and it was like living a new life, one that didn't involve going out, doing our daily routines. Now we were limited to walks to our neighborhood or neighboring park.

When the WHO declared a pandemic, it rocked my world into the new realization as if I need to improvise, adapt, and overcome this new transition in this new normal.

In an egocentric way I was fighting to get it back. Get what back? The previous lifestyle vanished the moment it was declared a pandemic, and I just had to accept this new normal against my will. Like, in the Canadian show *Schitt's Creek* where the Rose family lost everything - their house and money stripped away from them - a trial and retribution even to get back up on their feet. It was kind of like that where my previous livelihood was a star peg trying to fit in the new hexagon hole of 2020, a kind of trial to readjust, to reconsider fitting into that hexagon hole replacing that star peg. Readjusting to this new life of a new normal, and there were growing pains to that, because it was so, so, so different.

But eventually, it'll be most likely to happen somehow in my life, unquestionably and inevitably, regardless of a growing pandemic or not, some life-altering realizations may or might happen whether I like it or not.

If a fortune-teller made an appearance in front of me and asked me whether I would like to know about my future, the fortunate or unfortunate events, I would simply respond, "yeah, thanks but no thanks. I would like my future to remain a mystery."

For instance, it would be scary to know your own timeline before it even happened, and it would be not very enlightening to just know what to do.

I do want to share about how I continued to learn while being in quarantine ever since the pandemic was declared that March.

Yes, I was adjusting to a whole new world, and it wasn't all shiny, shimmering, splendid, like how William Shakespeare once said that 'all that glitters is not gold'. Being overly positive is good for a day or two but trying to keep maintaining that positivity is like refilling the same coffee filter almost every single day of being quarantined and still trying to put on a shining, shimmering, splendid smile on your face.

      Day after day, this new normal didn't involve the previous daily routines. It felt kind of being in the worst Stephen King movie ever, where the walls felt like closing in on you and you're wearing a warm cashmere or just a plain yet comfy sweatshirt staring out onto the window to the outside world. As if you're Evan Hansen in the wrong kind of movie.

      But in this day and age, we all have phones, and we all have Facebook, Instagram, X, and Threads to share funny memes or just beautiful photos of sunsets or sunrises or just even photos, or video, or thread posts (not so much related to the pandemic but some) to cheer each other on.

      Something to ease our minds and to distract from what's really going on, not to pretend this pandemic is really not happening, in which it is happening in front of our very eyes, not easing our minds, bodies, and spirits in these strange, difficult times. Yes, Mr. Shakespeare, all that glitters is indeed not gold and that is OK that everything you seek isn't as pretty as you expected. I'll be telling the future generations in my older age about me surviving, as if I were in a dystopian, apocalyptic world; but in reality, I was sitting in the house comfortably drinking coffee or tea, in a nice, comfy onesie and positively trying hard to make the very best of being quarantined instead of letting myself go insane.

I think, in this new situation, neurodiverse and neurotypicals alike had so much in common in how we were feeling in adjusting and adapting and overcoming this purgatory of a new normal. It's just that we neurodiverse don't know how to express how we truly feel about adjusting to such a very new environment.

*Did anyone really know how to express how they felt?*

It isn't our fault that it is super problematic to express how we truly feel instead of just bursting into sensory overload fits. For me, it's like a *Google* search that is frustration-inducing as if I'm stupid enough to not know what the F is happening. It was the worst feeling to have as if I were having some kind of a panic attack, but I didn't even know how to express that from time to time. I was repeatedly trying to tell myself that it is OK and it is also OK to feel this feeling, just let it rush through me like a rushing current of water of a creek right after it rains.

My aunt and grandma figured I could benefit from therapy, and they signed me up to talk to a therapist with whom I met once a month.

There was a rather good thing to share about having the extra time and being kept in the house. Yes, I was trapped in the comfort of my own home. In some ways, and now, sticking to the point that it is an oddly good thing to be kept in the comfort of my own home, was that I did a lot of writing (this book!) and reading and also, learning the soft skill that EFRW could never teach me, and that was cooking. Cooking as in using the oven and using the stove, in which I worked my ways into cooking myself omelets and I even cooked ratatouille with my aunt in person and over FaceTime a few times. After that I was hooked on cooking and baking with her. I baked and cooked. Baked some goodie treats, such as brownies and then tried to bake a bundt cake, but it got stuck onto the pan and we turned it into crumbly, yet still delicious brownies.

  Over time, I've realized that while still in this weird, oddly stressful time during the peak of a pandemic, I intended to shake out the negative uncertainties and needed to do things to leave my mind from the unpredictability of this new normal.

***

  Adjusting to that new normal felt like two things. One, it is an introvert's dream and two, it is also like Jack Torrance overlooking a hotel from the dead of winter to the first day of Spring. I'm sure in the future when my generation is our parents' or grandparents' ages, the talk of 2020 and being kept in our houses would sound even more epic to the next generation than it really was. Like, we all were in apocalyptic clothes, driving in sandy dunes as if we were all in the universe of *Mad Max*, but in reality, we were all wearing one-hundred percent masks and stood six feet from others and were home in comfy onesies, reading a book, binge watching a show and baking bread made from scratch. Even though this was not a laughing matter in the heat of the moment of the pandemic where we all had to wear masks and be safe, both physically and mentally it was like more of a Pixar movie rather than a Disney movie while being kept quarantined, I was more internal within myself.

    I wondered how other neurodivergent people handled being kept in the comforts of their own homes without sensory overload every day. It's hard enough to have to readjust to this new normal but one of the fine prints of being a neurodivergent is the difficulties in having to go through abrupt changes. Not all of us are so slick to accept abrupt changes and it is not just us neurodivergent who feel that way. Sometimes the world doesn't revolve around us as if we are the sun and everybody, we dealt with is the earth, orbiting around us in about three-hundred and sixty-five days, 24/7. This may sound harsh but yet it is only me, one pal's opinion on how we think the world revolves around us on a regular basis. Thinking that our struggles are harder than others' struggles. Like I once said, all people, autistic or not, are all different yet quite the same but each slightly unique.

  We all have our own journeys. We all have questions we ask the universe that not even the wise old owl in a tuxedo and a monocle would have the wisdom to answer. It's OK to not immediately know the ultimate future plans of yours, it is especially OK to travel down your own road in order to figure out what you truly want. And if you stumble across a crossroad, that is the luxury that deserves the utmost appreciation: to be able to stumble on a crossroad. To stumble on a choice between two choices that are going to change the outcome of your life when others often don't really have a choice.

  Twenty-Twenty, the pandemic and being quarantined for a year was like a blip that wasn't meant to happen. As if the Infinity War was real and after Thanos' Snap, half of our future plans for 2020 just disappeared into cosmic dust and the half we have left was the new normal.

  *Was this a lesson that needed to be learned?*
  *Was our life something we all took for granted?*

  This narrative may turn from a positive note to a somewhat negative one, but what is a good life story without including both the good, the bad, and the ugly that'll make my own story richer and turn it into a 3-D movie, valued more than just 2-D? And it is just so true in a way that it is not really an option to choose either the happy, sad, or just the mediocre side of life in how I tell it in my true, brilliant, unique way.

What my aunt would tell me is that happiness isn't just given, just granted, it only happens when I work on my own happiness every day. It doesn't just come and go, it just stays six feet under now rushing to the surface, not fast but slowly. Maybe that is why I'm so drawn to this science fiction book that was written in 1931 titled *Brave New World* by Aldous Huxley, where a society in the future where everybody in it is *truly'* happy and the idea of family has been destroyed. Living in this kind of lush yet lustful world where everybody is conditioned about what they ought to do is pretty horrifying in many ways and other emotions like the states of being sad, mad, angry, lots of varieties of different emotions were discarded, and only the state of being happy was accepted. They were keeping and putting happiness on a pedestal, like a model, a rulebook, a guide to follow to be happy.

And yep, I've nosedived into the rabbit hole of 'Brave New World', holy crap! I'm so drawn to how the people in 'Brave New World' lived and how they hang out with each other and how those people are made, conditioned and are never born naturally, out of another human body. Recently and currently, this same topic keeps ringing into my eardrum, high into my cerebellum, located near my limbic system: what it means to be happy; it is not something given at the time when I'm born, it is a feeling that keeps and needs to be worked on and that's a relatively good or bad thing. It's almost like the idea of the different types of OCDs, there are no bad ones, not relatively good ones, too, they're relatively OK ones. I can't really select my mood when I wake up every morning, I only make sure to run the day instead of letting the day run and stumble onto me. Sometimes it is more than I ever expected from the time I hopped out of bed to being fully dressed, sitting somewhere with a cup of coffee and a laptop in front and northeast-ish of me. Sometimes the day is like the currents of a river and I'm on an orange raft. Swiftly getting thrown side-to-side, unlike a peaceful stroll, other days a crazy thrill ride and I have the choice to control myself or tip myself over. Each day of quarantine, being kept in one location for a long period of time was hard enough and also felt like hanging on a thread and in the orange raft all in one.

    That was the other thing I've learned from being kept in the one and only location and either a phone or a laptop in front of me, is to be a coffee filter, enable any difficulty I've faced, letting it absorb and flow through me from head to toe in acceptance and grace.

## CHAPTER 24: - THE GREATEST MILESTONES

In the movies, it's easy to watch something with a desired outcome, but how and why is it inevitably harder in real life.

I don't buy into the wholesome concept of 'happily ever after' because I don't really believe in that BS. I know everybody, including myself (obviously) wants a somewhat desired outcome that we all see in movies and on television. But we can leave that to Hollywood.

'Happily Ever After' is just a justification of the idea of a perfect bow ribbon wrapped around a book so fondly, so beautiful, making it so flowery and cute that we all get giddy with glee and excitement, wishing for any of that to happen to us in real life.

The kind of idea that is so fondly burned into our brains to ever think so childishly, thinking and relying on the fabricated, mushy, lovey-dovey fantasy we all have in common.

A milestone ought to be reached by a certain age, they say. But that is not always the case with neurodiverse people like me.

I had my fair share of doctors who just made

poor judgements and assumptions about who I would be and what person I would become. Some entered my life as if they were Grover Cleveland and I was the five-year-old Franklin D. Roosevelt. Those types of Cleveland people wanted to tell me that I could never be anything or that it is too hard, in my situation. Yes, it is hard, but never 'too hard." I try to avoid people that only break down my confidence, brick by brick. I choose the right group of people that are on fire, the same way I'm on fire, which will make things worthwhile.

  I do believe in milestones, but I also know that it'll take me more time to reach them. It's not that I'm mentally delayed; it's just that that turmoil hasn't got there yet as a revelation, a breaking point. Like my incorrect diagnosis by that doctor, who thought I wouldn't walk, talk, or think, it was just an assumption, like the strange wish President Grover Cleveland wished upon ten-year-old Franklin D. Roosevelt.

  People believing that I can't and the focus on the can'ts started when I was born, brought to this world. It took one doctor who made a guess on who I will be in my lifetime, thinking that I'll be not capable of the basic human tasks.

  It started from a crude doctor who I proved that she was very wrong.

  Proving others wrong has become my specialty, for when someone ever dares to make assumptions, or thinks I can't do something, now, I'll be like 'no, no, let me try'. That all started from my own reflection from a mirror, pulling myself up to walk. Sometimes, a milestone is definitely worth the wait even with all the turmoil I have to go through.

I walked with my peers in 2018 with an Applied Studies Diploma and that was also a milestone in itself. Then, two years later I received my full High School Diploma, and nothing would stop my path. Now as I look back, it was like climbing three mountains at once and I'm happy and forever grateful for my family and the teachers who believed I could get there.

Those milestones became my own personal sorcerer's stone that transformed all the bitter work I've endured, and I could look upon them with a gleeful smile.

Yes, I do feel insecure and do feel being judged in hindsight in who the F I am, as an autistic and a person. The only thing so incredibly cool and amazing is how my brain works and thriving on out-of-the-box ideas. To that respect, I do think like a YouTuber but also have wildly abstract imaginations.

Somehow, over and over, I've been thinking that I'm on the middle of a bridge between neurotypicals and neurodiverses in the way I think and the way I do things,

        That'll only makes me
          happy. Happier, truly.

    It's just that the only thing stopping me is the insecurity I have and hearing the mini, judgmental voices in my head, questioning the way I think, the way how I view the world and the way others perceive me that

        I'm just a try-harder,
           or just a punk trying to get my name out there.

## CHAPTER 25 - WHAT BEING AUTISTIC MEANS TO ME

"I've always done whatever I want and always been exactly who I am." ~ Billie Eilish

When my mom first told me about my diagnosis as a teenager, my grandma was worried that learning this information would perhaps bring me down in despair. In reality and in my favor, it wasn't the tip of the iceberg the Titanic hit, instead it was just a revelation, an 'aha' moment, an answer to all my questions about why I'm the way I am.

Knowing that nugget of information it didn't break me, or shatter me to bits. Instead in the long term I think it made me stronger. Like what Kelly Clarkson would sing, "what doesn't kill you makes you stronger" and I stood "a little taller" with some notion of unexpected pride in myself. I got this far being autistic. That positivity would never change despite the news of my diagnosis, I did not let it happen. I did have to shake out the negatives in order to see the positives. They don't always cancel each other out. I love reading or watching success stories where they share both the 'not-so-good' sides intertwined with the 'obvious, good, happy' sides because with a good success story comes hearing and learning about the bad.

For instance, is there a certain way autism

should look like, so others could know and detect it, to know the difference from neurotypicals versus neurodiverse; to detect it so they can place me and put me in a little box somewhere in their minds to better understand? People never actually ask me about my autism. It's as if the topic was taboo. I'm however like a robot, scanning and trying to detect telepathically what they're thinking or saying about me, about my autism. Yes, I was diagnosed with it and yes, I desire to call myself identity-first, instead of person-first.

I'm an autistic person.

I don't look autistic or maybe I do? Some seem to sense it. Is it the way I walk? The way I talk? Is it how aloof I appear? I'm not sure. I'm also a human being with a brain, veins, and with a mind and feelings, so I'm broad and unique. Autism is a spectrum, not a mental illness or a plastic Target bag that you carry around like you're an extra in *Gossip Girl*. Autism is part of me, it made me who I am, because without it, I would be a completely different person.

Autism is like my body hitting a growth spurt, making me feel skinnier than I already am and sometimes I need to hide it by wearing baggy clothes.

I try to hide my autism, not only because I'm insecure, but it makes me feel like an alien fresh out of the spaceship from a totally different planet and I try to think like a neurotypical and I improvise and adapt, in order to overcome. Not that I'm ashamed of it, it is who I'm and there's nothing I can do about it, all I can do is to embrace it with grace and accept myself fully.

 The crazy thing is that I do feel like a wooden star-shaped peg trying to fit in the circle of society and its status quo and yes, neurotypical or not, it is hard, hard as I'm Olivia Rodrigo looking out saying "god, it's brutal here!" (from her song "Brutal).

 There was a metaphor that I beautifully used for myself to kind of find clarity and help me stay grounded.

 I'm standing on a bridge.

 Hear me out, a bridge.

 In the middle of this man-made yet magical bridge in my own mind, me standing on it by myself.

 You may be wondering oh, gosh, in horror, but it's not that at all. I love life and there are many, many highs, many, many lows and yet I can't let the small things defeat me.

 I stand on this bridge and simply admire the sunset in my own mind, a gentle breeze of the wind and a smile on my face. A genuine smile, a kind of smile that I snap a selfie for Instagram for clout and attention, a genuine, wholesome smile.

 The whole scene in my vivid mind is so beautiful: it's a simple tune of an acoustic guitar of an alternative-slash-indie song.

Me standing on the bridge, leaning over the barrier between me and the abyss below, then looking straight to that imaginary sunset with a happy exhale.

Then, I look to the right of me and see a piece of land attached and that is the lush green land of neurotypicals. And on the other side is a much smaller desert, the land of the neurodivergent.

I want to be part of the lush green land, but it is hard for me to find my place in that world, not because I don't want to be there, but because of society's expectations. It's absolutely hard, but worthwhile trying.

I'm not going to sugar-coat the fact that life is hard and that's what makes it so unique and special.

*But what is life when it is not hard?* That is a question that answers itself, based on my own levels of perceptions. It was answered for me, gradually and not immediately. My grandmother once said to me that if everything was easy then everybody could do it. We all have our very own strengths and weaknesses.

And I agree with her completely, because in some other way, life is and will be hard but definitely worth trying. It's definitely like stepping out of a high school classroom and being sucker punched. The reason why I used the bridge metaphor is because it helps, it soothes me to understand my own place in the world.

Yes, I do have autism, but I do think like a neurotypical, as if I'm a Folgers half-and-half coffee ground, but still coffee.

Half-neurotypical, half-neurodivergent.

It's a part of me, not a part of me, that can be stripped away; it is who I am. I'm always in the middle in-between neurotypicals and neurodivergents.

For some reasons it feels right for me to not always know where I belong, even in the way I behave around neurotypicals or neurodivergents.

I feel mixed emotions when I'm in either group: in one we can commiserate but I feel I don't want to be there with people with a worse condition than I. It's not their fault, they are doing nothing wrong, it's more of an issue I am dealing with. In the other group I feel excluded, like the bouncer before stepping into an exclusive nightclub is holding up his hands to me saying "No!"

*Excluded how?* Excluded as in, I feel insecure when I'm around neurotypical people, because I'm often ignored. How I think to how I process things, and how I view the world, yeah, I feel different from them.

My grandma points out, that I am missing the "mean" chip which many people seem to have in their brains. Since I never speak up about how I really feel (Ms. Murray is not aware about my disdain for her and I doubt she will ever read this book); I would never want to make anyone feel bad about themselves, never have, never will – and since I am not picky with what food is served to me or what activities to participate in with my family; nor what clothes to wear; since I never complain and I am the most easy going person, my family says that if all people were like me there would be peace on earth and all the ills in the world would disappear.

Autistic people aren't clones of each other, it's wrong to think we are all the same, that we all think alike, or we all process things the same way. Neurotypicals should give each of us a chance. We are all different, just like they are each individuals with their own values, feelings, personalities, goals and dreams.

That is why I accepted myself, little by little, placing myself in the middle of two lands, one lush, one a tundra, two worlds, two planets, two universes, as if I'm the Avatar.

A bridge between the spiritual and the material worlds.

## CHAPTER 26 - IS IT REALLY MY CALLING?

A new road awaits.
A new road ahead.
Onward onto the new road less traveled ahead.
Forward, not over it, is what lies in front of now not behind.

Now, you readers have reached this point of the book. Congrats! Now, I will be continuing to tell my story of the moment my own lifetime clock struck 13 (and this isn't a George Orwell book).

In May 2022 with the pandemic almost in the rear-view mirror, and all my shots up to date, I was accepted to a state-funded training program in western Virginia for food service. I was so excited. Because I cooked countless times during the pandemic with my aunt and her fiancé and experimented with spices in sandwiches using Naan bread and spreads with hummus and baked delicate cakes, I really honed my cooking and baking skills. I felt I have somewhat of a calling about being a chef and my mom and my aunt agreed that this food service training program was a perfect idea for me.

So, I went to the training program and it's a pretty cool place for people on the spectrum, where state instructors are training and preparing us for being in the workforce. It wasn't my first time there, I had gone there in a previous program for about eight weeks when I was in high school, the bygone years of not having to wear masks and socially distance ourselves from others from an airborne virus that changed the course of our charts, made us take the hugest de-tour that was known to men.

So, I started this new training program in 2022, just barely out of the pandemic era but still had to wear masks and stayed in a separate room for hygienic and safety purposes. The first few weeks were just orientations. We were getting used to what was expected in this food service program, working in the little cafe which served only the staff of this overall place. They were familiarizing us with the terms and conditions that come along with food services.

This little café serving the staff of this overall place felt a bit strange. Strange, how? Strange in a way until it dawned on me that the two people in charge of the café and running the whole operation were mainly interested in pleasing the caregivers of the autistic, not in us the autistic people who just wanted to learn more about the culinary arts.

Now, the caregivers of autism, not just the autistic people?

Allow me to explain. Some people in this world really have the intention to teach us neurodivergent people about what's required in the real world and how to deal or cope with the neurotypical in a rather healthy way. But others don't even bother to give a sh*t to change the environment around us to make it somewhat comfortable. Those types of people feel that accommodating someone's special needs are too high maintenance as if we were A-list actors and actresses needing people to work for us to get through daily life. And if the instructors are rude to us and we are rude back, they will play the *I'm-a-grown-up-don't-talk-me-that-way* card.

    So, I had mixed feelings about this program, because yes, I sure loved the independence of living in my own dorm – I did my own laundry, my own cleaning, chose my own food at the cafeteria whenever I wanted (and quickly gained twenty pounds) and I slowly got out there in the community - slowly. My mind was still in the pandemic era. Slowly but surely, I was adjusting to the post-pandemic world.

    Weeks passed at that facility, with lots of overviews and training when I finally got to cook something, but not for myself to eat (I would on some future days) but for the staff.

    I do remember the one day I was finally the dessert person responsible for making chocolate cookies. That was so much fun. It made myself feel so good as if I were in the British Baking show and I proudly showed off my tray of cookies. My instructor, Ms. Murray, turned to me and rolled her eyes. "By the time you're done with one tray, I'm done with 20." Hmh? Well, good for you. So much for the fun of a British Baking show.

As the days progressed, and I got further into the training, it wasn't all enlightening at all and became very stressful.

For instance, one day I had to bake an elaborate cake, and I was asked to find the icing in the freezer. Now finding something in that big freezer was like getting over the biggest hurdle of my life and then falling off into a hole right next to the hurdle. And when I asked for help saying, "I can't find it, can you give me a hint where it could be?" Ms. Murray looked at me as if I was a complete utter imbecile.

"You have to learn to find these things yourself you're not helpless."

Shrunken to the core, I went back and continued to search every shelf, every part of that freezer. I could not find it.

Over time, feeling her stares in my back, Ms. Murray grew more and more impatient and just pointed where it was supposedly located. It would have taken her a few seconds to actually get it herself, but she insisted to point with an irritated look. Finally, I found the icing. Next, she needed the pie crust. Still agitated from trying to find the icing, I went back to where she was pointing with her shoulder and a look in a direction – I think she was pointing towards the fridge, again. But I didn't want to ask her any more questions.

This moment was the catalyst, the breaking point, in how I perceived Ms. Murray. Finding that pie crust became my nemesis and was my biggest challenge and for some reason it was always located at a different place. That was part of the training, it seemed; can people with autism find what we are sending them to find?

I was so stressed because not only did I have to find the crust but there were time pressures. Find it now, or else the cake will not bake in time. It will be wrong. It will not taste right. On most days I was very stressed because Ms. Murray still didn't bother to come and actually help me even after a long time when I couldn't find it.

One day, when I finally found the crust after a specially long time searching, it left me no time to prepare the pie and Ms. Murray acted all disappointed and with a deep sigh said, "No one will be happy that they won't have any chocolate pie because of you!"

The ultimate breaking point for me was when she pulled out slices of leftover cake as back-up because the pies would not be done. As if she had planned the entire spectacle. I felt anger boiling, runneth over, but I managed to put on a lid from seeping out, but I was seething. She hid the crust so well but then blamed it on my poor time management.

That was her verdict. I had poor time management. She used that to justify her side of the story, making it her words against mine.

A little later after that whole debacle, whether I was in my dorm or on a daily walk, seething under my teeth, I was in a battle within myself, gaslighting myself into thinking, *was it me who messed up the pies?* or *was it me who couldn't find the stupid pie crusts?* or *couldn't she have just shown me where the pie crusts were?'*

At the moment I didn't even bother to write down how I was feeling, because that really didn't occur to me to do so until my aunt and grandma encouraged me to "write down your feelings."

I did that and quickly learned that writing my thoughts down is another form of therapy to help better yourself and to reflect on what happened to you; and to be encouraged to do so from the mouths of family members helped a lot. Because they're the only ones who love you for who you're and have good intentions to encourage you to write down on paper something that seems very unfair and detrimental to be able to move on with your life. It was definitely encouraged by both my aunt and my grandma to write down how I was feeling that day with the infamous search of the pie crusts to get them out of the rivers of my head and onto the thin sheet of paper and the sound of the slam of a book to exhale the last final negative breath about the event. Just breathe, they said; in 5 times, out 5 times, while counting. I would 100-percent thank them a thousand times for mustering myself into writing those journals to get the thoughts off the mental space in my brain so I'm able to move past it, even though it's also suitable that over time I resent the person that caused me mental harm the most: Ms. Murray!

    I felt that this place where we went to learn skills before we stepped onto the brownstones of the real world was half-downright awful, despicably so. Some of the staff and the instructors were just rude rather than blunt, and they should be thinking twice before cutting some pretty nasty looks at me that made me want to hide and stay in my dorm all day. Some of them do mean well, seriously, I know I can't really fall into the category of a young person who just wants to speak out just to speak out or I'll just be perceived as a snowflake. A very sensitive one. But I'm not, I'm only just voicing the absurdity of this overall place that may seem a bit outdated and stuck in a time wrap, the '50s or '60s perhaps.

    Weeks passed and it felt that I had lost my passion for learning more about the art of cooking, because my being there was clouded with resentment towards Ms. Murray. She wasn't just mean to me, but also to some other students in the food service program and I did feel pity for them. The reason I felt bad for them is that they didn't know how to feel angry at the right time, they didn't know how to voice their opinions without Ms. Murray throwing around the you-don't-talk-to-me-that-way card. *Why is it that staff or instructors always have the upper hand even if they are rude?* Really sad to say the least, which is always the case between students and anyone much older than us.

    *Is it about respect?*

    *Or is it about power?*

    Yes, all young people should respect their elders, anyone much older, because they have lived much longer than young people and have more experiences in their lives. And I 100-percent agree, but here's the catch: anyone much older in order to gain respect they also have to treat us respectfully. I mean, is it too much to ask or to wish and to fight for a hopeful future of a world to be comfortable and sustainable for all to live in and not making it harder than it needs to be. And no, I'm not bashing anyone older, only the way some act arrogantly and selfishly and some are just miserable. I do feel that, yes, they are experienced and have a fair share of regret and made mistakes that they are just looking out for in my generation and younger yet to come, and I'm forever grateful for that. But is hiding a piecrust to teach time management the best way to pass on that knowledge?

    ~

My mixed feelings about this overall training place in southern Virginia, near the University of Virginia areas grew stronger towards the negative. One day I was called into a meeting. When I got to the room three instructors were sitting around the table. They asked me to sit down. My family wasn't informed, so I had nobody to back me up, and I didn't know what this was about. The lead teacher Mr. Brown started out by saying:

"Lewis, you don't really want to be in food services, do you? It's a high-paced job and I'm sure that's not something you want. Imagine working at McDonalds and you have to fry burger after burger. Would you be able to keep up? No siree, I don't think you want that?"

He had a good point; it sounded good to me at that moment. After all they are the adults who have my best interest, right? Before I could think about it any further, I agreed with Mr. Brown, of course I wouldn't want to be in a stressful McDonalds environment.

My grandma would later ask me, "Did you self-advocate?"

There was that word again! I think everyone working with neurodiverse people knows how hard it is for us to self-advocate, to stand up for ourselves.

But my grandma explained later, that it was Mr. Brown's nice way of letting me down. Before I could even think about whether all that was true – did I really feel this way, did I really not want to do food services anyhow? – I was told that I no longer was allowed to continue the food services training. Out of 20 people applying to food services, two were not accepted and I was one of them.

Maybe they are right, maybe I'm too slow for food services, but I'm also very sure that the teacher didn't have enough patience for me. My grandma thinks it's because I still had all my rights and I was still making decisions for myself. Many of the other kids can't make decisions for themselves and their parents have to weigh in; their parents have the "power of attorney." That's how three instructors could call me into their room without me having any other representation; no family member was there to defend me. Though, I understand I should self-advocate.

That week when I wasn't accepted into the food service, it struck a chord with me that even if you feel qualified as a cook and you feel it, heartbrokenly others may not see nor want to see it that way. I think the only reason that Ms. Murray didn't accept me into her precious, little food service was because she didn't have the patience to teach and did not want to deal with someone like me always messing things up. And she did seem that way, the cocky, egotistical, prideful type, who's too darn good at her job and often bragged how she's been cooking and baking since she was young and how she could make twenty cookies in the time I made one. That's not teaching, that was just making me, and the others feel super sh*tty about whenever we messed up the recipes and believe me, I've tried my hardest and it wasn't enough. Duh, it is patience and learning curves and clearly, she didn't have ounces of patience and good riddance. Ms. Murray tried to break my love, my passions, my purpose for cooking and baking because of how many times I've made small mistakes and she thought, 'why bother teaching him? He's an imbecile.' Oh, no, I wasn't. Again, she just didn't have the patience to teach me, and I guess quite frankly she's too smug and arrogant to teach others anyway because she bragged on how great she was at the whole thing. Well, good for her, but not so good for me and others around. And the crazy, bizarre thing is that when I bumped into her in the hallways before working with her, I never thought she would be a totally egotistical, horrible person. She seemed nice.

 For a short time, I was thinking of quitting the program altogether. But my mom and my aunt told me that in real life there will be many Ms. Murrays, and I would just have to learn to deal with people like that. It was all part of the training. I needed to see this through.

 So, I had the choice to seek out a different training path: housekeeping. That week was extremely hard for me where I felt I was spiraling out of control because Monday I found out and around Wednesday or Thursday that week I went for a walk thinking through everything that happened. I was festering and festering wondering what I could have done differently to pass food services. What were the other 18 students doing that I wasn't? What was wrong with me?

I looked up from my thoughts across the field and there was a huge dog running towards me. I was so deep in my thoughts about flunking food services that my first reaction was to run. I now literally was chased by a crazy dog outside of the walking path near our center. I ran as fast as I could and was terrified to the point I tripped and fell onto the gravel and scraped my knees badly. It wasn't to the point that I needed stitches, but the student services nurse put on so many bandages where it was challenging to walk. Oh, boo-hoo, you don't need to feel bad for me; I relive that moment of being chased by a crazy dog now every time I see a dog running and not on a leash; it shakes my very core. Small dogs I can handle, but those big ones, nope.

I reached the peak of my stress. Well, at least I thought I did.

So that oncoming week I had a vocational session for housekeeping to finish up with a heavily bandaged knee and I was a fighter, and I did push through, that was annoying, but I did it and the vocational part was very easy. It was just the instructor throwing down dirt on a rug so I could vacuum, and he purposely messed up the counter and the table, so I could clean them in detail and even set up the table. Those vocational classes were easy, and I finished up very quickly. When it was all said and done, I knew what needed to be done and what's required of housekeeping because I helped out with the dorm cleaning. The food service possibility fell through, but another rose up, another opportunity. And that is the beauty of life in which high school doesn't really teach us the realistic hardships of life, just a bunch of sappy lip service. A lot of things that do need to adjust for the better, starting with the education systems for both non- and autistic people in schools to learn more about life more realistic than just studying Shakespeare. But in other ways, young people understand the misleading truths to seek out the real truths, because it is worth discussing. Even though much older people do have the experiences and their fair share of mistakes in their lives, it doesn't mean to show cockiness and spitefulness towards the young, assuming that they all know nothing.

But I'm still so glad to get out from underneath Ms. Murray's grip and into something new like housekeeping; out of the distressing woods and into the clear meadow to deeply exhale. That's the thing, when I said this overall training place gave me mixed feelings, mixed emotions, because there were some things I did love and enjoy and mostly it was independence and some instructors weren't a\*\*holes and wanted the complete best for me in life, respectfully. I would walk past that cafe opposite my housekeeping classroom and just scoff and see the other students learning the art of cooking.

On the outside looking in, respectfully, resentfully.

And the other sad thing was when I was kicked out of food service training, the other students didn't seem to miss me, like I was always an afterthought. I just vanished without them knowing, or didn't seem to care. Some did say hi to me, but that was it, just 'hi', 'bye', and we walked our separate ways. Yes, I got the message, the intentions that I wasn't welcome back into the food service, but I certainly didn't get closure because I felt that it wasn't justified that they thought I was not qualified to learn about cooking.

Again, that week seemed to be one of the worst weeks of my life and there were some chains of events that happened to me: being chased by a dog was the straw that broke the camel's back because I was so stressed that I wasn't really prepared for life's rejections. The thing I wasn't prepared for is that others so simply- and single-mindedly cannot see your potential, or even have any patience to help you grow and your life will be altered because of their crappy decision. Which that week nearly shattered me like if I was a Nokia phone, one drop onto the ground, breaking sounds, broken, cracked. But I was so glad that after the one option crumpled the other opportunity rose from the ashes like a phoenix and that was when I started housekeeping.

At first, when I started housekeeping, it was just me helping out with one of the dorm cleaning staff and there were only two people running the cleaning staff, which was very impressive because there were many dormitories. But I mostly cleaned outside each window and each trash can around the dormitories and on other days when one of the dorms emptied out, one of the cleaning staff taught me how to clean the rooms in preparation for the next person coming and also to clean the showers. And I felt happy with this new environment because there at the food service I felt that I wasn't happy or evolving because the soil was like the sand in the desert, only growing cactuses. I was more like a hibiscus, growing better and striving on the ground in a warm climate. The only problem about this whole food service debacle was that the environment wasn't suitable for me to grow and flourish like a hibiscus, or a gorgeous flower ready to bloom because the soil wasn't for me at all. Even though I tried to plant my own seeds and replanted them into the uncharted soil, but it wasn't suitable. It was scorching, piping hot, way too much sun for my own seeds to just be roasted rather than break through the ground.

So, the housekeeping program felt that it was right for me, because we all on the spectrum are special in every way, we are all unique. We can't just lump everyone on the spectrum and make the assumption that we all need to be handled in any crappy circumstance or situation the same. That's also why this vocational place to teach us the ways of the world and how to behave in it in order to 'be-fixed-into it-BS.' It's a mistake that a comfortable world is not built for all of us. Any unnecessary background noises aren't so easy to drown out and yes, we do live in the iPhone era, and everything is consumed by technology, but how can we change it? The world is just not built for us people on the spectrum, and that's not something for neurotypicals to be upset about. But our challenges are all on the bottom of the iceberg, and neurotypicals can just see the tip of it, we people on the spectrum live the tip and the bottom and that is what we're advocating for. Advocating for a world that is currently just not built for us.

A lot of things that happened to me at this vocational place that I was not proud of and that I had to learn the hard way:

    1.    Not be accepted into the food service
    2.    Being chased by a crazy dog, which was at the peak of my stress about not being accepted into the food service and everything

surrounding it.

And yes, there's a third (and maybe a fourth) that'll take the cake.

It started out a normal, chill Saturday and I signed up at the Recreational Hall to be able to go to Target like we do every Saturday to browse around and then go to Starbucks and to just get out, get away from the campus, because it could get a little boring seeing the same things all week long. So, I went to the bus with the others and did the usual at Target: I grabbed my Starbucks drink and walked around in the movie section, looked at the CDs and the books aisles but that day I also checked out the clothes aisle. As I do often, I also went to the snack aisle to treat myself to a case of double-stuffed Oreos and it was that day when I thought of buying Christmas wrapping paper. I was thinking of making homemade paintings in my dorm for my mom and dad, aunt and grandma, and I would wrap them with the wrapping paper I bought.

But after I paid, I thought I could browse some more, just look around some more but all of a sudden, I realized it was almost 4 pm. I rushed to the front of the building. There were no other students with the same kind of lanyard as mine and no bus that had the vocational place logo on it. I started to panic, went in and out the store (not the smart thing to do) until a Target manager noticed me and went up to me, asking me if everything was OK. I told him that I was left behind, in my most fragile state of mind. So, after I talked with the manager, who suggested I call my family, I called up my aunt and her fiancé to let them know because my aunt always comforts me, and I knew they would know what to do. That was the most frightening afternoon of my life and what was very odd was when the Target manager tried to call the people on campus the calls went straight to voicemails every time. And it was getting darker and darker by the minute, and I was starting to get really anxious, but I did have my aunt and her fiancé on the phone the entire time to guide me through this scary experience. So, the Target manager had an idea and that was the only last resort and that was to place me on a Brite bus that connected to the campus, because the phone calls to the place trying to let them know that they are missing one student still went unanswered. My grandma had recommended an Uber or Lift, but in that rural area there was no Uber or Lift service. So, that Brite bus was the knight in shining armor and luckily, I could ride on it for free because the Brite buses had some connections with my vocational training place.

      I was both grateful and terrified while sitting on the Brite bus because it was pitch black out and I wasn't able to see where it was going and all I had to go for was my gut feelings. The gut feelings were like 'is this bus taking me back to where I need to go?'

And finally, I got back to my campus in one piece, I was so relieved and thanked the bus driver a thousand times in gratitude. So, I got off the bus and my aunt and her fiancé who had stayed on the phone with me this entire time, it seemed for hours, instructed me to slowly walk towards the cafeteria to check and see whether dinner was still in session, in which my gut feelings told me that it might have closed, but it's always good to check. Then I had this overwhelming feeling of fear wave over me that when I set foot onto the Recreational Hall to the cafeteria, that I would see the person who took us/the group to Target and that he would spot me and give me the meanest, stern look that would turn me to stone if he laid eyes on me. So, I slowly walked into the Recreational Hall and I saw the person who took me to Target but luckily he didn't see me and I thought in relief 'oh, good' because I couldn't afford to have my head ripped off and another stressor enter my nervous system. I checked the cafeteria, and it was closed so my aunt and her boyfriend ordered me pizza for dinner, which I was both grateful and embarrassed that I had to bring them into my own messes. But, nonetheless, the past is in the past and that night will still hold a very problematic stain like a spilled coffee on my cleanest, silkiest white bedspread, but it'll also help me reflect on and grow. Yes, I was just left behind and it was a very scary experience, but I had made it out of the woods in one piece and another resentment enters my resentful pot about this overall vocational training place. That this place is so stuck in the 20th century and can't even pick up the F*ing phone whenever a student has gone missing.

My grandma and my mom wondered how this could happen. My grandma called and sent multiple emails. One to Target Headquarters

*Dear Target Management,*

*I wanted to write to you about a Target manager in Waynesboro, VA, named Nate. A very nice young man, who deserves to be recognized, as an angel among us.*

*My grandson is autistic and yesterday afternoon a bus from a nearby neurodiverse training center where he is attending training, dropped him off at Target there. He and the rest of the neurodiverse folks were allotted a certain amount of time to shop as is the case every Saturday and then the bus would take them back at 4 pm.*

*For the first time he has gone on these outings, my grandson lost track of time in the store and got back at 4:05 pm. To his horror the bus had left without him. Being neurodiverse and being far away from home this is a very complicated scary situation for someone who is autistic, and he was visibly shaken and scared, pacing up and down trying to figure out what to do.*

*The young Target manager Nate noticed him being distraught and walked up to him, asking him how he could help him. My grandson explained his situation and Nate sprang into action calling the center, but no response. Nate then asked my grandson calmly to call his family who then texted us and we then also stayed on the phone with him. Nate stayed with my grandson in person the entire time and calmed him down. Then Nate looked up the regular bus schedule and noticed that a bus that stops at Target also stops at the center. Together they waited for the bus and Nate never left my grandson's side inside Target, who was also on the phone with his relatives. My grandson got back safely to the center, and he has learned a valuable lesson to not lose track of time and to set an alarm. I would like to award Nate with a gift certificate (where to send - we live 3 hours from there) and also am hoping that you can recognize Nate somehow for this service to the community. People like Nate restore my faith in humanity, and he is truly an angel among us.*

*A very grateful grandparent*

She even then called the store to talk to Nate at Target to thank him personally and because it was close to Christmas she wanted to offer him a Christmas gift card or anything he could need.

Nate told her he wasn't looking for financial

compensation, he said he only did what's right. He also said that he is so very appreciative that she sent a note to Target HQ and the note got back to his manager and he was praised by his manager and his manager said that's a pretty big deal. And Nate said that's all he needed is that we showed our appreciation that way he said that made him happy; he is not looking for money or financial compensation that's not why he did it.

    There are some really nice people out there.

    My grandma also wrote an email to the vocational training center:

> *I hope this email finds you well. I just wanted to pass along what happened this weekend. The bus from campus dropped Lewis and others off as usual at Target Saturday. He and the rest are allotted a certain amount of time to shop as is the case every Saturday and then the bus would take them back at 4 pm. For the first time that Lewis had gone on these outings, he lost track of time in the store and got back at 4:05 pm. To his horror the bus had left without him. As you can imagine, this is a very complicated scary situation for someone who is autistic and he was visibly shaken and scared, pacing up and down trying to figure out what to do. A young Target manager Nate noticed him being distraught and walked up to him, asking him how he*

*could help him. Lewis explained his situation to him and Nate sprang into action calling the campus, but no response. Nate then asked Lewis calmly to call his family; Lewis then texted us and we then also stayed on the phone with him. We gave him the emergency number at campus that was provided to us, no response. We called there also. No response.*

*Nate stayed with Lewis in person the entire time and calmed him down. Then Nate looked up the regular bus schedule and noticed that a bus that stops at Target also stops at the center. Together they waited 1 hour and 15 minutes for the bus to show and Nate never left Lewis's side inside Target, while also on the phone with us. Lewis got back safely to campus and he learned a valuable lesson to not lose track of time and to set an alarm. When he got back nobody had noticed that he was missing on the bus. He also missed the dinner time.*

She got some kind of response of how sorry they were and how this has never happened before and will never happen again. And how the driver has worked for them twenty-seven-years and he will make sure to do a better head count and… and … and...

My grandma said they were nervous we would take this public. But she said nah, why bother, she was sure that bus driver learned a major lesson as did I.

The day after the Target fiasco, I decided to

just lay low in my dorm and just relax after a stressful night. And I had noticed a low but striking pain on my side, like a constant pinch and thought that was weird. And days later it developed strikingly into serious pain and when I told my aunt and her partner they took off the day from work to come and they had to drive for over three hours to get me to a nearby hospital to figure out what was going on with my body. After a long process in the hospital, the doctor told us that my colon was inflamed due to the foods that are served to us – rich and creamy full with butter, just how I like it - and maybe the peak stress from that Target fiasco. But mostly the food I ate was unhealthy. We didn't have much food selection, though there was a tiny salad bar but that was not enough. Most of the entrees were deep-fried and delicious but as my aunt said they will clog my arteries and have me slowly develop some health problems. This was towards the end of 2022, where I started to have to watch what I eat every day, not just making it my classic, traditional New Year's Resolutions. A resolution for the new year doesn't have to start by the stroke of midnight. You can start it any time and it'll get easier to maintain in the new year in the most utmost and definite way possible.

~

*On making friends:*

I just wanted to say that making friends as an adult is so F*ing hard much harder than it was making friends in high school.

*Why's that? Why is it so challenging as an adult versus when I was in high school or grade school?* Maybe there's a sense of belonging, a certain people that had their doors open wide to you, so inviting and you're in and you felt like the most important person in the world. It was a time in my high school days where social media were definitely in, but not like in 2020 when Instagram first launched Reels that made the app more like TikTok and that I sometimes wondered if Reels had come out in 2018, it would have made my high school days even more exciting than just traditionally posting photos on feeds and on Stories.

Okay, getting a little side-tracked but yes making friends is more challenging as an adult than as a teenager. And I find myself more frustrated and my family rolling is rolling their eyes when I choose social media over real life people to be friends with like that choice isn't an option. The reason I choose social media over most of the students at this overall vocational place is that they are just very odd to be around and most of the time they are either in their dorms or just being odd to me.

Not me in front of me, but my mind reads odd in general.

And they are all on the spectrum some more

some less.

And also, most of the activities in this vocational place don't really draw the students. There are card games and board games but none hold and keep our attention longer. Not that we all have a short attention span (we do) but still I do feel that the staff should really amp up their activity games here. You know, like open up a social media club and talking about how to post without being an egotistical a**hole or practice safe social media use. And the only time we leave the campus is when we go to a movie theater, Target, or Walmart but nothing else really. One time we went to a nature trail overlooking the Valley, which was fun. To that I would go again and again. But they only offered a hike once. They just need to broaden their horizon to just make it a little tad bit better instead of being stuck in a time warp of the twentieth century.

And I do find myself rolling my eyes where older generations oppose the idea of social media, saying it's just an app. I know it's an app and so is Facebook. Oftentimes I wonder how older people just brag that they can and led double lives more flawlessly than Hannah Montana to have an online life and much more *real* and *physical* social life with "*real, physical people*" in this 'real, physical world'. As if I am Olivia Rodrigo with my arms crossed and mouthed *good for you*. I know that social media is used for people to post their everyday lives, the highlight reels to their accounts are always shown more happy, vibrant and with groups of people with wide-open smiles that look more fake than genuine. And effortlessly made friends, like it's so F*ing easy.

      I do know that it is important to get myself out there to make friends with others and some people do have the best intentions, but at the moment it appears I'm happy just choosing social media and I'm not even trying. On the surface, it may look like I'm not even trying, but burrow deep, I'm trying my ass off. Trying to say "Hi" to someone walking by who doesn't even acknowledge my existence. Trying to go bowling with someone when nobody is interested.

      And I know that it is a computer, the pot calling the kettle black, all generations use social media, even if it's just Facebook. But you know it is how it can be used, not just an ego-boost, like a drug, but something it can be also used to connect and to tell stories visually. Why can we all be both happy and uplifting on social media and also in real life? Open a whole new conversation then just shutting it down by spitting at the monitor, making it not work. Like, discussing a new way in how being introverted is actually a good thing rather than just a horrific thing.

      Also, in the beginning of the pandemic in 2020, while everything was in lockdown and there was nothing else to do but just kept up at home scrolling, on online classes and watching the same shows and movies and going on nature walks to maintain a healthy mental outlook added to the way I'm today: a bit of an introvert. I still do love to talk to people, but it drains me after talking to them and I do take is as a compliment, a reward to myself that I took the liberty to speak to someone after trying to recuperate from the isolation of the pandemic. And even when I was younger, elementary school-aged, I was a bit introverted. You know, I kept things to myself and oftentimes lived in my head, imagining myself on a stage audibly dancing, singing to the song *All For You* by Janet Jackson. So, it isn't really a surprise that I'm the way I am today, withdrawn, but society loves to make it seem that being an introvert is a terrible, terrible thing. Like, dramatically putting their hands over their mouths, dramatically gasping like that's the most monstrous thing a person ever does being an introvert.

  Think of an introverted person reading on a park bench in the pre-social media era. That person chooses to read books rather than having to interact with other people and is blissfully unaware of their surroundings, trapped in the pages of a good book. Fast-forward to 2024, where books are around but social media is very, very in and some people choose social media the same way as that person on a park bench chose a book, newspaper or magazine, pre-social media.

That society just wants to demonize the things they don't understand so the concept of being an introvert is somehow a rocket science concept to grasp. They often look at me who seems very, very outgoing from what they see on Facebook and Instagram but when they meet me in the real world, I come across very different from the person online. It's like a weird way that society was being catfished with the intentions of me being the most real I ever was but only on social media. I post some pretty real content and try to demystify topics that aren't so easy to shake in the real world and online try to have a better, clearer understanding of those unshakeable topics that somehow society has trouble understanding. The moral of the story: don't just quickly assume the person you meet on social media and that person you met in real life is a lot different than what I brought out online. Online I might just dare to be myself. Check me out on my social media, and you will see.

And yes, social media is the most amazing world building experience ever made, and it doesn't have to serve as a totally egotistical framework. Not everything you see online is always an ego just wanting to be fed, it can be a place to demystify topics that people in the real world don't know how to talk about and that's worth talking about. Many people just love to fixate on the negatives of it all, saying that it is not good for your mental health but that's the 2% of it. 98% of it is an experience that feels broad and wide. That I know it is an app or a computer but there's no F*ing denying the fact that social media can open many doors that are mostly positive. And we are just creatures of habit who love to use it in the darkest of times but in the most click-baiting, toxic positive posts with smiles so fake they seem real. Maybe that's why many people choose social media over real life people because real life isn't as bright and happy as what they imagine online because real life can be oddly dull and colorless. I do know we do need that dopamine to meet with real people and it can boost your confidence level to a high but drains you after hours of talking to them. Just give yourself some grace and patience and drown out the noise of society placing on you about making friends and just do the things that make you fulfilled and happy, in your own terms and pace.

  Making friends isn't going to happen overnight, but overtime, little by little, step by step, you will find what you need in moderation rather than trying to cram everything into one expectation that'll make you truly happy. It's just going to make you more burnt out like a too long candle wick burning too high. Making friendships doesn't have to be a chore, but you can prioritize how it fits you. And my mind is still in the 2020-pandemic era mentally and yes, I would say that the pandemic had changed me to the gray area between better. Almost like I'm listening to some songs from the Taylor Swift "Folklore" and "Evermore" albums, wandering mindlessly in a deep, tranquil forest, mesmerized by the beauty Mother Earth has offered and captured from a photo or a video from a phone.

~

After that day being left behind at Target and then being diagnosed with an inflamed colon after the ER, my aunt and her fiancé took me back home to my parents to stay to recover and start my quest to eat healthy to manage this inflamed colon. I thought to myself *great! Another con to dislike about this overall place!* But it was a good thing that they took me back home to heal instead of continuing my housekeeping training and still eating those unhealthy, fried foods.

In some ways, I'm so glad it happened to me because it was a little buzz of a wake-up call to start eating right and watching what I eat and still enjoy a good diet. Eventually I would crave other things than burgers that would be special and worthwhile. During that period, I had to cut back on caffeinated drinks and only drink decaf. I know, the horror! I also cut back on the 3,000+ calories intake that my body used to have at that vocational training place. I trained my body to not always crave very high calorie foods but instead eat in moderation like a small entree and a side of salad or go crazy during lunch and go light on dinner.

I'm not saying that going on a diet was super easy, oh, my god it really wasn't!! It was life-altering and life-changing and an eye-opener to take better care of your body!! In some ways I'm not kidding, it's super hard.

Temptations are what makes it super hard, like a wind chill on a wet cold day. Winds make everything worse on an already cold wet day. It's so hard to actually put in the work of watching your figure versus just saying you're going to watch your figure. It's so much easier to say on paper "I'll do it" than actually putting in the work. Figures! Yep, try to keep your healthy diet when on a trip to Disney World. It's super easy. Not!

That was a long winter break for me, mine came easy for me when I had to come back home to recover from my inflamed colon getting worse and I'm forever grateful that I have a family, the ones who showed me what food to eat that I could eat to both maintain my figure and keep my colon from getting more inflamed. Families are islands of people, a tribe of people that hunt and gather and who love one another instead of resenting and being spiteful to one another. I know no family is perfect. No one is perfect, the picture-perfect family doesn't exist. That's only for marketing purposes to see photos of families, happy, blissfully happy families where you're buying a new picture frame, but no families are the Hallmark cookie-cutter cut-outs models. Families also are not here to criticize out of spite, but out of love and the intentions that are good even though it might not seem that way in the first given moment, but in hindsight. Something that my mom said to me days before I headed back to the vocational training place and it stuck with me like super glue was along the lines of *although you have a disability that shouldn't ever be the thing to justify not achieving what you want.* Like I can't always live life by just using my autism as a flotation device in swimming in a sea of safe waters, preventing me from drowning. Life would throw something at you that you may not like. There are unchartered waters.

    Either trying to catch the life vest, or just let it smack you in the face.

    Autism is valid.

    Autism is human.

    This got me thinking that the reason I'm writing this book is to have a clear understanding of my past and present journey and also to have others treat anyone on the spectrum with respect, not like they are "special." Because many people on the spectrum are different and not hard to differentiate between autistics and non-autistics. Let's say someone on the spectrum can't speak/is nonverbal but has a device that'll help that person communicate with others. Number one: have extreme amounts of patience and listen to every automatic word coming off the device with care and curiosity. In this case, it's OK to make an exception in treating that person in a special way but with respect, because that's true: Respect is everything whether you're nonverbal or verbal. Other people that don't have autism should not treat anyone with autism like a situation that needs to be handled, or a circumstance that needs to be squared away, but treat them as people, just like the rest of the others in the world. That is what we are thriving for and fighting for. For acceptance every April, don't only have an autism awareness month, but also make it about acceptance. Maybe 'awareness' for any areas who don't know what autism is and to slowly educate others about what it is instead of fear-mongering, adding to the awareness of the falsehoods and misunderstanding of autism.

    So, that's what my mom said to me that sometimes I have a disability but can't use it to justify every little circumstance in life thrown at me. Again, I'd rather try to catch or just let it smack me in the face, yes boo-hoo, it'll hurt like heck, but I rather not try to dodge life in every way shape and form though. It's better to learn from getting smacked in the face than trying to dodge it to get away from it and it'll hurt because you'll learn in the future that the next time you just have to catch anything that life throws at you and learn from it.

    Because we on the spectrum, are in this

world too, but anyone not on the spectrum trying to have us adapt to that world could be detrimental.

We are human, too. We can handle any given setbacks and negative feedback thrown at us. We aren't special species of people that only act like we're weak but in reality, we are so far from weak. Others just haven't seen it yet or just quickly assumed.

Like society treats women, we are second to that list.

The feeling of not reacting quickly enough and letting it bottle up inside until – we won't let it explode but sizzle out.

And not being taken seriously. All the things that happened to me in the past are now being spoken into this book because at the time I wasn't emotionally mature enough to know what those feelings were at the moment and it's not all fluff, puff-pieces for a magazine.

Again, let's not make every April an 'awareness month' but also an 'acceptance month.'

Actually, it should be every day rather than just one month to be accepted for being different from the rest of the crowd. I know it's the intention and most of it is good but just throwing out 'Autism awareness month' leaves a pretty bad taste in my mouth. Like every June with pride month, some companies love to throw in the rainbow like its paint, splattering it all over the wall, the same with the color blue for autism. I heard that 'lighting it up blue' isn't really a thing no more. Why's that? I'll tell you why. The color blue was associated with autism while the world was a bit sexist thinking that only boys could be autistic not so much girls. Was it just an incredible masking by girls to not be able to be diagnosed with autism or is less expected of girls or is the focus on boys? At an early age boys were easier to diagnose with autism, why is that? Changing from Light It Up Blue to another color that associates positivity and that is also not triggering. Like green or yellow or even a rainbow and not a puzzle but an infinity symbol that reads that it is a spectrum, not separation of different types but a spectrum, not a dichotomy. And also wanting to change from the infamous blue puzzle piece is like how Taylor Swift is re-recording her old six albums and rebranding them (Taylor's Version) in how we want a rainbow infinity symbol instead of the puzzle piece associated with autism and the color is now red instead of blue. Red includes all genders and red shows there is a fire within us. Awareness on social media is one way but the other way is to donate to many autistic organizations that research autism and speak for autistics not against and use social media to bring any uncertainty to light to demystify, to understand, to spread the word whether through humor or storytelling. But it's more than just demystifying the misconceptions of autism to make it clearer, more than just being viewed as parasites just thinking that we only drain our families' resources, but really autism is more of a neurological difference than a disease. And more than just stamping the infinity symbol, the colors blue or red, so aimlessly and mindlessly, actually donating to any organizations that are for both the autistic individuals and their families. The best of both worlds.

~

So, I got back to the vocational training place after a long winter break. I know right, I still couldn't believe that I would be back.

I'm so glad that I pre-started one of my New Year's Resolutions about eating healthy to manage my figure and keeping my colon healthy and also it makes you feel amazing to have a slender body. Not too fat, not too skinny. Just right. But it's OK if your body is either fat or skinny when you're healthy and proud of your body, that's what matters.

But I was still having trouble making new friends and always choosing social media over real people. What's so wrong to do so because maybe some people are a bit odd, but I know that isn't a good enough excuse to just be in my dorm and not hang around the Recreation Hall. I found it kind of funny that many students there always stay in their dorms even if I'm out of my dorm and around the campus, trying to bring myself out. I do know now that making new friends always doesn't have to be a chore, it doesn't have to be required at all. What it does take is a lot of grace and patience because you'll slowly attract other people. Post-pandemic me is no joke because my introversions were amplified while being in lockdown, although I was an introvert, which explained how I once was in elementary school, pre-social media, in the playground, and trapped in my imaginations.

  Being an introvert is not as terrible as others make it out to be. Society just loves to paint pictures that they really understand, when they don't understand something, they just shed a light of misconception. Like when watching those true crime documentaries on Netflix, they always say that the the suspect seemed very quiet, had no social life, no friends, and was reserved and kept things to him- or herself. But not all introverts are like that. It's not as terrible as people just make it out to be.

  Think of it this way: your brain is like a lighthouse that serves to warn or receive any kind of vibe or signal that another person you're almost about to meet is giving off: a weird, awkward vibe. That'll help you guide with believable small talk and a cheerful 'see you tomorrow at the same time' like a boat not going to close to the rocky cliff into and out the harbor. Very simple: either STAY AWAY, DANGER, BEWARE, or COME THIS WAY.

Because you'll know what that person or myself are going through, a hard day at training and reading the room: 'I'm tired, I'm drained, don't talk to me until I feel fully refreshed'. You never know what the person is going through and just wants time for him or herself to recuperate after a long day. That isn't selfish when it's based on self-love. And also, what's so crystal clear in my mind is that don't just quickly assume anyone on social media is as bright and bubbly as shown. Take it all with a grain of salt, because it's funny to say the least that no one, I mean, no one wants to see anyone who posts about wallowing in their own self-pity online.

  That's what makes social media very convoluted because people scroll and always see the positive highlight reels of others' days and most of them are about the end results of baking a cake, not the entire process. Or always seeing the end results of improving one's body weight, they don't really include the whole process but just the results because some people don't really want to see what supplement you used or what food you didn't eat to manage that amazing body. That is also why people love to fixate on the negative effects on social media, because they're only focusing on the positive highlight reels that put these things people want to achieve on pedestals that give high hopes to the point that they just get burnt out and resent the social media app. And social media doesn't have to be used for egotistical purposes at all, it just doesn't have to be that perfect. It could be used for serving purposes, problems that could be demystified for the better to better understand them rather than just condemning them. And also try to add the process in baking a delicious cake instead of filming or snapping the end results, because there is a shift happening in the media where people do have real, raw materials on their feed, not the light, fluffy puff-pieces as if they are being curated for a fashion or those entertainment magazine, because that is so 2016. It's good usage to inform someone about something very hard instead of just vanity posting.

    It would be scary and quite personal to share things intimately online and so casually, I mean don't share anything way too personal but only things that feel true and raw and authentic to you. Like an audio you found that speaks to you and use that to tell something raw and real.

    Because part of the definition of insanity is vanity, in my mind.

    So yes, being an introvert is typically hard for me, but I know that making friends is important and good for your mental well-being, but it shouldn't be a chore and a number one top priority. Not something to stress out about, but just to work on continuously because I'm sure that others can relate to that. Making friends as an adult is not as easy as when we were in high school or on papers.

## CHAPTER 27 GOOD INTENTIONS OR GASLIGHTING?

You're probably thinking while reading this book that I've dealt with a lot of negatives in my life. That's true, but it's not that I'm causing a scene or just wanting to create drama because somehow my mind loves to make everything seem like every person is out to get me and always has the worst intentions of not wanting me to move forward.

I often perceive a look from a person's face as a single attack, for example a simple eye roll, or a simple tone of voice can set me off thinking that the person is being snarky with me without even realizing in the moment that it could be that's how that person always talks. And yes, there were some people that were more kind to me than when I was in that cooking vocational class, the whole experience there was terrible, because the instructor didn't have any patience whatsoever. But I know now that sometimes in life that I will have to encounter those types of people, whether I like it or not, that'll only give me more character and remind me that not every person on this earth is out to deliberately cause me problems . There were also some positive things that happened when I was at the vocational training place. In 2022 when I had gotten out from quarantine, the few days there were an adjustment from being in COVID lockdown to venturing out.

One little problem was  where the pandemic made me an introvert, but it is just that my confidence may be blocked according to public speaker Mel Robbins. And now I do think of a new way to use the word confidence' as an action, not so much of a feeling and that is so enlightening and a total eye-opener.

        Those eight weeks at the vocational training place, called Prep, were the best eight weeks of my life where I talked to some people. I met some people who also follow me on social media which it's a good way to always stay in touch. Prep where I learned with other students learned about how to get into a job and to be respectful, to self-advocate, and to communicate to my very best, although it is not my strong suit, like math isn't either. And on every Thursday, we would all go to the auditorium to watch movies based on our own circumstances that'll make us feel seen, heard and not alone. The reason those eight weeks were the best because it was refreshing coming out from lockdown but we still had to wear masks to be safe but it still felt freeing to venturing out and to find your mark, your place in the world and how to be a member of society, even though your circumstances are quite newly and vastly different than others. But that shouldn't always be the case to use that as an excuse but to accommodate to advocate to tell your future bosses and co-workers. What's life if you're always saying that your circumstances could just be used as a floatation device or some kind of a barrier to keep yourself getting hit in the face while sometimes an experience wouldn't kill you but make you stronger and build your character development. It'll be just boring and a not-so-great way to live life that way.

    In the past, I would take any looks or any unintentional tone as an attack, but now I've also been telling myself that whenever a problem isn't too big. It's a waste of energy to get all worked up. Too small to worry, just a brush off the shoulders like *that doesn't bother me much* at all. It was also good that those negatives happened to me in order for me to rearrange my thought process and reshape it from negative to positive thinking and always say to myself that in life there will be people way mean. That will be unacceptable but sometimes whenever it feels we want to change, to fix those kind of people, it's just not the case. Always look at it as if they are just having a bad day, something happened with their families and their emotions snuck out and you saw a sliver of that even though they checked their emotions at the door. But they are human after all and have beating hearts and it is normal to let out emotions when least expected and it's not always towards you at all.

    Even though it feels good to try to change their unacceptable behaviors and it's not the 'woke' culture, it's just human nature. It's good to be aware and to be communicative in how some people are rude, but not all people just wake up every morning and are just a total sour-puss from the get-go.

Just take things into perspective.

Sometimes I do wonder if the people surrounding me actually have good intentions in telling me that I can't or can't do anything I put my mind to. Like when I'm in this vocational training place or just in general, I wondered if the people who're training me for the real world do have good intentions.

Ninety percent of them really do have good intentions and aren't out to get me, pulling me down dragging down my own self-worth. The crazy and annoying thing is that I let that other small percentage, the other amount of negativity circle around my cerebellum like the moon around the earth and the earth around the sun. For instance, let's say I want to be a barista at some cute, quaint coffee shop, working with the coffee machines but someone walked up to me and tries to convince me that it would be a very hard job to do and the way this person words it to me like the person really meant well, thinking that I couldn't handle that kind of hard job . In that case, I do cave because that tone of voice is like a trance, hypnotizing me into agreeing with this person. After all they mean well, right?

That can be frightening for someone on the spectrum by wording things into making it seem that others have the best interest at heart and using a tone of voice that is not too harsh because we don't do well with a harsh tone of voice, like we're utterly clueless children. And the most frightening of all is that I then agree and cave without further voicing my opinion that perhaps working at a coffee shop would be worth trying out. And this definitely happened to me when I was in high school, in those special education classes where a teacher used that tone of voice saying that I would not want to work at someplace like Starbucks and I did cave, and agreed that it would be hard to work at a place like that. Without me even trying it out because I would never know whether it would be easy or hard, like the label 'autism' to some is like a Scarlet letter but less depressing than in that story we always had to read; to use that kind of label as making it seem that 'oh, you have autism and you're challenged so you're limited'. And I just know that I cannot live up to that depressing, soul-shattering narrative and that there's more to autism and thinking I'm not a fraud.

    The reason that I think it's gaslighting is because I would say this is what I would like to do, and they would say " it's too hard". , Would it be this detrimental to an allistic person i to be supportive? Would it be the same to tell an allistic person that perhaps they shouldn't even try something, the same way as being told to an autistic person? Like, if an autistic person wants to be a lawyer or a doctor, they would be saying to them after sucking air through their teeth with a disapproving look on their faces, implying that'll be a tricky career choice not worth trying. They'll be like 'oh, being a lawyer or a doctor takes several schoolings' as if we don't know that already in acting like some things on the spectrum we are limited in our own knowledge. And I do know that some people aren't always out to get us, pulling us down to the abyss. I do know that the people on the other side do have the utmost good intentions in achieving something you want in life to be happy and not letting our minor circumstances get in our happiness. By thinking we autistics live up to the puzzle piece mentality, and all we are thinking is that there's a piece missing within, an empty void needing to be filled.

 Not true.

 There are different ways in filling that void in positivity and in finding your inner peace and inner warrior to shake out the gas lighters and definitely it's hard to detect them. Like ripping the rug beneath my feet. And I'm not just saying that to justify that due to my own autism but being able to read the subtle nuances and social cues to a gas lighter and their intentions and actions. Yes, being a lawyer or a doctor is a hard career choice, or even a barista at a local coffee shop is hard enough, but what a gas lighter doesn't know is that it is worth trying. I know I would never want to be a lawyer or a doctor, those were just examples for me to convey but the barista bit was based on true events.

Some people treat people on the spectrum to be babied and act like they can't be treated like the harsh realities in life don't apply to them as well.

Like they are so special.

Not to get it twisted, there are some people on the spectrum that need way more guidance given their circumstances and lack of understanding of social cues but most of all it isn't really their fault at all. More guidance to better understand the cues surrounding them rather than excluding them, thinking they would grasp 90-percent or less. Like at a dinner party and friends who happen to have kids separate them by two tables: an adult table and a kiddie table, where the adults talk about big-boy-big-girl topics while children talk about fart jokes. They are more like kids playing on the iPad with their headphones on. Don't underestimate a child with headphones because even though their ears are plugged in, you think they wouldn't hear, think again, they can.

I do also believe that the difference between people on the spectrum who need more guidance than those who act like fully capable people in the working world or just in life in general where people with more guidance often justify their circumstances but if a fully capable person on the spectrum does the exact same thing, it's hiding behind his/her autism. This would sound mean but it's quite not, it's like just giving those with more guidance a trophy for just breathing and existing, but again, I know deep down it's not their fault. It's just that they can't easily detect and regulate their emotions the same way another person on the spectrum would.

    In the training place I was in, a student gave a very interesting and eye-opening revelation about the difference between acceptance and being tolerated . This student went by the name of Jake and that revelation cracked a nugget of wisdom into my cerebellum. During Autism Awareness-Acceptance Month they do a walk around the quad that looked like a wide, rectangular courtyard. We all - a total of three students - stood to watch the speeches a few students and some teachers gave. One of them was Jake and we met when we were in food service training. I do respect his ways and wisdom; despite the fact that I wasn't accepted the food service, but that wasn't his fault.

    Towards the end of his brief speech, he mentioned that people should tolerate us and then try to accept us because it is canceling the tolerated stage and goes straight into acceptance. Tolerate our perks, quirks, and our uniqueness that makes us much more strangely different from the rest. Out of respect, we do jump towards acceptance and skip past the toleration stage, thinking that's all we ever need and thrive for. What Jake said really cracked up my skull with this new wisdom about toleration and he's as wise as a wise old owl trapped in a twenty-something-year-old body because it is very true. We should thrive for tolerance for who we are instead of just the 'good intentions' to spread the word. Even though spreading the word is just stage one: wearing shirts about respecting autism and just two colors that will associate autism: red or blue. Or using the puzzle piece or the infinity symbol without leading any actions after that. In order to accept autistic people, we have to tolerate our quirks that society may find weird and abnormal but is normal to us instead of making us look like we're hiding behind our autism because we all know that we do have potential, we just have different ways to show it.

For instance, I don't think it's really fair to justify some autistics who need way more guidance because they *can't handle it*. You don't know what those autistics go through, how they are thinking and how they should handle things in life. Again, it is not their fault they're like that, but that shouldn't be the only justification for being the way they are.

Is that hiding behind their autism, or me hiding behind mine?

I don't think it's hiding behind my autism, it's more like knowing your limits, knowing how much you can do - how high or how low. Other people and I on the spectrum, rather than hide behind our autism, we try to mask our autism. It just seems we suppress ours to look more neurotypical to societal norms because for some neurotypicals it's abnormally weird to witness for them to handle so we mask ours to feel included and accepted, but not tolerated. And this isn't for you to feel bad or myself feeling sorry for myself, but have you best understand our minor, little struggle we endure in you thinking it's not so much of a struggle but a shameful pity-party. You probably think this is a rant, it's really not, more like a TED Talk than a rant, to address something that feels like injustice. Yes, autism is neurodiversity, it's a spectrum, not a dichotomy between two sides: fully capable and the need-more-guidance, but just changing the name from autism to autistic to neurodiversity is not going to make a difference. Yes, it's nice to reinvent something that used to be there to not make the word 'autism' or 'autistic' a taboo, a dirty word, or just something dreadful. Trying something new and fresh with it, having a new spin on things to shake things up but the actual autistic circle won't be any different if you change it or not. Even with good intentions.

What's neurodivergent to some of you is still autistic to us.

For people with autism, it requires excessive patience and deliverance for them to ease into the hardcore reality of life without triggering a sensitive overload. *Why just give up learning? What makes an autistic person tick? Well, carpe diem, bitches!* Seize the day to make your life as extraordinary as Robin Williams would say it. Regardless of being neurotypicals or neurodiversity alike, carpe diem to all for the current times to trailblazing futures, because we are all the same people.

These photos of my times as a kid shouldn't be used as the green light for Gatsby, almost like memorabilia, a token of lessons learnt but to only recap and both admire and appreciate my childhood greatly.

Forever grateful, where I once was on the road less traveled by and now focusing on the road to new destinations. Using my own past as a passport to pass the borders to my near-or-far future goals and dreams, not to just recall them, but revisit and relearn from it.

Like I said in the first chapter, looking back in retrospect makes a huge difference in my own life. In hindsight and in reexamination, it's very beneficial compared to where I once was in my life to where I'm today, appreciating it. Appreciating where I once was is like quickly admiring my own journey of the past, but not wanting to relive it. Recalling it is just a Gatsby thing, for me, it is like walking on a nature trail with the sounds of birds chirping while the sun's rays are shining, gleaming onto the outside my face and inside my head which is empty, drowned in thoughts. In thoughts of my own timeline, both honoring and praising where and when I stand today in such blissful, grateful and appreciative matters.

    Looking back in retrospect isn't a symptom of Peter Pan Syndrome or how Jay Gatsby approaches the green lights, wanting, begging to recall a time in his life to reality. Looking back in retrospect means admiring, honoring, appreciating the small, simple things in my own life, which play a huge role in my own agenda. Looking back onto the past can also give out some pretty important lessons that were learnt as a child now retaught as an adult but seeing the bigger picture from those life experiences and lessons.

## CHAPTER 28: "WHAT LIES AHEAD OF ME"

"That best portion of a good man's life, His little, nameless, unremembered acts of kindness and of love." ~ William Wordsworth

At the beginning of my life, I thought life was a movie, we are in a movie, but as I went through middle school, high school, being a super senior, then the training I realized life is reality, harsh reality that I have to deal with daily.

I do repeat myself a lot, because in the past, I've had people who just discarded what I just said. So, now, I always have this notion in repeating myself just to make sure that someone got what and heard what I've said.

In the first chapter of this book, I've mentioned that looking back into the physical form of my childhood and this is a photo album and revisit in the dusty corridor side of my brain, recap my own memories like it is a television series. I do know that constantly viewing my own childhood memories would only make me feel super delusional and questions of what is the past and what is the present. I sure do know that to live in the moment is certainly inevitable, it's there, it's 'in the now.' The present, where the duration of my own childhood or what happened a year or two ago is over and the only thing begins the present, every time what starts and restarts the clock. That cogs and gears of my own timeline continue tick-tocking, recording its new record, and there is no way to reverse it back to a time of myself back as a kid. But, admiring just by receiving a smile on my own face when I recap my own life, appreciating where I once was and where now I stand, made me think the roads I had traveled, some crossroads, that led me up to the current road I'm on here, today and in the present.

  Someday, I do think when I discovered my own autism, that just fully made me answer my own question of my own alienations. *Why am I like this?* For instance, *why do I feel so different from the rest of the pack?* Those were the questions I had asked myself before I was told about my own autism. I was told that when I was a bit younger, my mom wanted to tell me the real truth of my own true self and colors, but my grandmother hesitated, thinking that it'll make me even more alienated than ever before. Until at the age of 16, I revealed my true nature and left me at awe it let me to the answer about my own alienations. Looking back is also like me looking onto the pages of my photo album of my captured childhood pictures and that only plants a smile on my face. Seeing happy, little me so blissfully jovial and so unaware of the world surroundings that the happiness in each photo I want slivers of them transmits into me into my adult self. Looking back also means that I'm learning all the things used to happen in my youth had shaped me into who I'm today. Yes, I'm autistic, but at first glance, people wouldn't see that side of me which wasn't intended to be seen.

Not that I'm insecure, but in some ways, it would seem that way, but in some cases, don't blow yourself into a charity case, to feel sorry for me, nor feel frightened about speaking to me like I'm an alien in a different planet, different galaxy.

There was a clear notion the moment I turned thirteen, it was loud and clear that I was (as the cool kids say) that I was woke. I was awakened to this burning knowledge that I do have more to bring to the table than just letting others feel sorry for me or for myself feeling sorry for my own self for being the way I am.

I know there is no syringe, no *cure* for autism, because autism isn't a disease, it is how the brain works.

And let me stop you right there, *why is autism treated as if it were some uncommon disease as if some haven't even heard of it before? Or like straight out of a horror movie where characters slowly grow more paranoid and turn against each other?* Almost like there are two types of flowers where one that can be treated, nurtured so delicate and it needs to be heavily cultivated and protected from easily shriveling up and the others are simple yet beautiful roses with thorns on the stems that are built for protecting itself from getting hurt externally that could and would understand the hardships of expectations of others of myself in who the F I want to be. I often wake up in the morning feeling a kind of pressure to mask out my own autism in order to fit into the puzzle peg of a star that society intends on fitting me into in which I could be a circle peg.

    It isn't something to be afraid of but there are stigmas for people who are diagnosed with Asperger's syndrome. For instance, labels that would help identify which are autistic or not, but it more likely grows the seed of insecurity more quickly because of the pressures of an autistic person trying to fit in. An outsider trying to fit in but feeling a certain disconnect to that of the same kind versus trying to fit into a new learning, friends-friendly environment. To me, it does feel like a blur between the Special Education and the General Education classes because when I was in the Special Ed classes, I felt like a swan in a group of ducks which felt so quackery and untruthful. But, when I was in the General Education classes with the students who don't have autism who saw me as the duck but for me, the General Education, I loved it so dearly because I certainly loved the challenges. I love something that'll make me strive beyond my own expectations, dismantling myself from the autism label. Back then, that word 'autism' for me felt like a life-sized sticker of a puzzle piece on my forearm, identifying myself in who I'm internally but slowly growing the seeds of insecurity into a grand garden. So, what I did was rip off the label like a band aid, leaving some hair off, dropping it onto the floor and stomping on it. It was a time where that word I believed was stripping me from striving and thriving into unchartered territories and I thought un-labeling and rebranding myself was the way to go. I replaced 'autism' to 'unique' because that was how I looked upon myself, looking at myself in a mirror and being like, 'you know, this is me.' Almost like on social media in calling myself the real' or something that'll uplift me, to reach that pre-existing nugget to existence.

    Deep down, I know I'm autistic and I'm not going to let a newly developed syringe to 'cure' autism be injected into me, changing me without researching more of the spectrum. There are more people on the spectrum who have different types of autism, and it is colorful, not black and white, but in between is a static blur line, dancing around like a no-signal, snowy television screen. In some people, in how they view autism, they view it as if the autism spectrum is like the old-timer television that only had three channels versus how another side of people view autism like it is a television with thousands of other channels with other streaming services. There are different varieties of what autism means and matters on both the inside and the outside. There should be more research and studies on how the brain of an autistic person functions, not belittling me with the label, or even just separating me from my own dreams and goals; slowly but surely oppressing, belittling my mind not allowing me to reach the heights beyond my own selves, limiting myself into not reaching new, unchartered territories.

For me, that rings bullsh*t into my brain.

I always have the instinctive notion to judge correctly before committing to something that could be out of my own elements. However, it is a regular thing of some Special Ed teachers who deal with being in a classroom with students with some kinds of intellectual, learning disability to belittle them in such a protective way.

I do know that the students with those learning disabilities often have accommodations like an Individual Educational Plan (aka, IEP) in order to help them strive to ensure the narrow path of overcoming an obstacle that feels so tightening. But it is mocked as a double-edged sword because it still has a burning feeling to it, almost like a burden, an unwanted name tag stamped onto my chest.

When I was in the Special Education classes, I felt that I was a fish out of water, on dried land, and not in my natural habitat. Teachers in those classes didn't see that I was uncomfortable, like I was wearing tight skinny jeans, but some of them seemed not to care.

I felt that I had some potential within me, and they just didn't see what I could do and just thought that I have autism and should be dealt with as if I were a helpless, little flower with thorns. Some other ways I did felt like I was a beautiful red rose with the sharpest thorns known to man, so looks can be deceiving. Yes, I do have autism but the teachers shouldn't define who I am, not allowing myself to define myself and not seeing that the other part of my nature is that I'm very sweet and often put my own needs aside to help out others.

Dumb down the high-spirited, including myself, because my challenges were so big, big enough to limit my own, true potentials. But I was destined to show them, to prove them wrong, cancel out my own autistic personality to something beyond, like overlooking from the ground up to see a metal bar too far up high above my head, analyzing how I should do it, letting my brain work its magic. Deep down along with the insecurity, I knew that I still have that fire inside that is building and roaring. Like a steam locomotive, fueled by a burning combustible and coal being shoved forcefully into it, continues to fuel my goals, my desires my dreams. That is what was inside me. Internally fueling my insides into analyzing a task or a challenge I see first-hand, fueling until I reach 100%.

It's sad how the education system just pushes young people to college or immediately into the real world like all the textbooks they have read and burned into their brains in school are going to help them along the way. Like I said, I love and admire the challenges and to fight back into getting what I best deserve, and I have the will, the drive, and ambitions that help me guide through that dark tunnel.

Addressing that *Everyone's Out to Get Me!* I've noticed how many incidents during this book where people I've encountered in my life were just mean and brought down my spirits. And often it appears I'm pulling this card of *everyone's out to get me, so help, help me, save me* and I felt the need to put myself in a corner to wallow.

Stupidly and immaturely, I've used my autism several times, blaming the way I'm for how people treated me, or what I thought they treated me in my own, sensitive head. From first glance, sure, they were mean, but some had some good intentions to do so and that I can't always let my castle crumble after one, minor inconvenience and then to use what those unfiltered people are showing and telling you is to get and be stronger.

It's good to address the mean people you've encountered in your life but always running out with tears, or crying on command, telling how someone was being mean or rude to you isn't the way to go. Because maybe the person who you thought is being mean or rude to is probably just unfiltered and super blunt and just says things in a non-flowery way and just says the things that need to be said. Because it may sting for a bit where we might think we are the exceptions, but the truth is that we are sadly not. We can still be unique and be ourselves in every way instead of just thinking we have to be exceptional, almost replacing that narrative entirely. Because it's going to make us feel a bit foolish to think, but in other ways if you think you're exceptional go right ahead and let that flag fly in the wind, it's your life, I'm just saying matter the fact. Because our autism can't always bounce back any bad vibes or negativities into thinking that'll justify the causes, like, yes, blame yourself or your autism for any wrongdoings you may receive but it may not help considering the fact that's now how the neurotypical world works.

 Like we're all a bunch of Barbies and Kens. What were we made for?

 I think it's that some mean people should be given the benefit of the doubt about their delivery instead of hiding ourselves in a corner wallowing in our pities into thinking like we're the victims. You know, criticism isn't being as if your castles are crumbling, and it does hurt to say the least with all the sticks and stones and bricks being thrown at you. But here's the New Romantics of it all: you have all these sticks and stones and bricks around you to build into a gorgeous, beautiful castle again. In the beginning and at first glance, it may hurt and may feel like a punch in the stomach but deep down you need, we ALL need criticism, and mean people to grow. And I do have this tendency to act like a victim and act as if everyone's out to get me, but I've been unlearning that nasty habit because it is not how I should live my life thinking that.

There are many other people in my life who uplift me like my family, my mom, my aunt, and my grandma, my dad, my uncle and more who help me unlearn those nasty habits. It's good to let in people who do have the best intentions for you and want you to succeed and to help out, even when it feels like an attack at first glance but in hindsight, inhale, exhale, breathe, relax, it's OK.

I'm like an infinity symbol, a different way of saying that I'm a jack of all trades, master of none. An infinity symbol that is constantly at crossroads; I don't know what I truly want in life, for the longevity of my own life. But my traits feel limitless, and I love to try new things and always put in the work and effort in looking into the mirror to look upon my own reflections - to see what I truly want. But, somehow, most people whom I deal with who want to say the opposite, always say the can'ts' and add up hardships to my paths, blockades. My family supports me and agrees with me, but society doesn't.

Again, what is life without those kind of

people?

Without those kind of people telling me the opposite, the 'cannots,' I wouldn't be able to thrive and turn the can'ts into cans.

The hardships to prove.

This goes hand-in-hand when in earlier chapters of my book I said that when I look at my own childhood photo, I see my past self still in motion smiling innocently and my present self looks down onto the photo with nothing but a smile on my own face. It brings me such comfort to see photos of myself as a child, seeing how blissfully happy and unaware I was of the state of the world at the time – I didn't seem to care, didn't know about my autism diagnosis, and lived in my own, little, happy world. Looking at my childhood pictures in my hand is another way to make myself proud and not to make sure to not screw up my future by making the wrong decisions. And if I do, I would be failing my own self, and I know that I'm being hard on myself, setting myself high expectations for myself, in what I expect of me. I have to make the right decisions in the right state of mind to benefit, to determine my own future. Sometimes it is hard to stay in tune, in sync with my own emotions but I know deep down it is better for my future to act on it positively to take it seriously. Almost like a complex villain in a show that felt angry from the start, dealt with redemption arcs along the way.

Destiny is just a funny thing that seems inevitable.

A success story that only contains the good parts but not the ugly ones isn't really a success story. That would be too one-sided. This is what I wanted for this book, to be a success story of my own, a type of story that is true to me and wholesome and accepts the awareness in who I'm as a person that autism became a part of me, not an accessory and the things I've had learned in my lifetime. Or not throw in toxic positivity to the mix.

For the longest time in my life, some other people didn't even know that I had autism and that just slipped past me like it's nothing. Deep down, it felt like something.

When I'm much older telling the future and younger generation about the times of 2020 and having to be in house arrest and wear masks and keep a fair, safe distance from other people, I would want to shine a light on what it takes to be a neurodivergent in a neurotypical pandemic world.

Probably the future, younger, more wholesome generation coming after me, prone to accessibility of technology, TikTok-scrolling of a large demographic of new generations of kids (picture this) a large auditorium and me on a stage, Ted Talk-style and hundreds of kids with their parents sitting in the audience. In my lifetime, I've been thinking how much the older generation just has misconceptions on being a young person without even fitting into the Converse, Avril Lavigne-style shoes, or just much more expensive branded shoes that aren't used for wearing than only just to display from afar. I would be on that stage talking to the next generation that the older generation in my lifetime were a bit unkind and just made some pretty awful or just slim assumptions on what we were, painted a picture in what they saw in us. I've been thinking that when I'm my mom's or my grandmother's age, I will vow a promise (and I know I cannot make promises that I cannot make and keep) to not make assumptions and misconceptions on the next generation after me and just accept them as who they are and just let them be. Just let them be, just let them be their own selves. Accept them with grace, into not letting myself paint a picture of what I see in those kids in the future, but just have the hopes that they would take on the responsibilities after my generation onto the world. I'm only tired of how the older generation viewed my generation as if we, including myself, would never ever take on the world, take on being the next governor, take on being the next US President, or just generally take on the world, to make it better for that next generation after mine. Yet both to praise and to be spiteful for what we do on social media, to create and to tell stories online. Nope, it can't be both, just one or the other: praising upon or just spiteful about said social media or off-social media.

    Historically speaking, we can't be all both praise-worthy then spiteful and fearful for the next generations to come to take on the world . . . We just have to trust their instincts and their ways of life because at the end of the day, no one's perfect.

    I optimistically hope and glad there's going to be a much broader future representation of autism than it really was in my youth. All age groups need to have some kind of human kindness and empathy and some human curiosity instead of just being plain judgmental, without not getting the full glory, the full scale of the whole, entire picture. Each and every one of them deserves some kind of deep cut understanding and wants to be heard and wants to be loved and above all, wants to be seen. There will be setbacks in a person's life and I can't always control how the world talks to or with me, this is probably mine and your journey, yours and mine, walking down the same or different roads, even if or when others from the side don't seem to understand. What I do know that those things such as wanting a representation of the diversity or anything that is not the norm, is not the beaten path for which society paved the way. Wanting to be heard, wanting to be seen, and above all, wanting to be loved. We all need and want that, and it is sad how some neurotypicals view people different from them as lesser as if they could not really lead happy and fulfilling lives. As if they use the puzzle piece logo to cover the extent how we all neurodivergents are and think.

Think we'll never be as happy as such.

Think we'll never have happy and fulfilling lives.

Think we all have a piece missing, a large portion, a large chunk of our brains missing.

But, no need to feel pity, or feel sorry for us neurodivergents. We don't need a party hat for this pity party, what we do need is a variety of accommodations to fit into this world that are not only fit for *normal* neurotypicals.

We aren't all different from the rest, but in some ways, we are all the same in our beautiful, brilliant, unique ways. We are all human.

Ending this isn't always easy, unless you're Frederick Douglass who wrote three autobiographies.

Writing this has been such a privilege telling my own story about myself being a neuro-divergent living in a neurotypical world, which feels that it does not fit me entirely and just not enough. The constant theme to this book is people I've encountered that aren't my family, are just strangers in this world, only making assumptions on how I should and could and would be. For instance, people telling me that I 'can't' rather than the I 'can', thinking that it is 'unbearably too much'. It's like how Walt Whitman said to 'be curious' but in the

Apple TV Plus show, *Ted Lasso* where he added onto a different flavor to the Walt Whitman quote is that Ted said: "Underestimated me my entire life. And for years, I never understood why. It used to really bother me. But then one day, I was driving my little boy to school, and I saw this quote by Walt Whitman, and it was painted on the wall there. It said, "Be curious, not judgmental." I like that. So, I get back in my car and I'm driving to work, and all of a sudden it hits me. All the fellas that used to belittle me, not a single one of them were curious. They thought they had everything all figured out. So, they judged everything, and they judged everyone. And I realized that their underestimating me... who I was had nothing to do with it. 'Cause if they were curious, they would've asked questions. You know? Questions like, 'Have you played a lot of darts, Ted?' To which I would've answered, 'Yes, sir.'" And I first heard Jason Sudeikis as Ted Lasso say that, it wasn't an automatic click of realization, instead I gradually realized it, like my brain was a coffee filter and all the hot water seeping, brewing over the fresh coffee grounds from head to toe.

  In the beginning, in the 'once-upon-a-time' era of my life, it would bother the heck out of me when people judge or just make assumptions about me rather than being curious and asking me questions.

  Afraid that I wouldn't be able to answer?

Afraid that I wouldn't reach your standards?

Afraid that I wouldn't be able to make a wholesome conversation with any person who stumbles upon me?

I think that is something many, many neurotypicals do with somebody beyond them, making the assumptions just on the way I walk, the way I talk, and the way how I perceive the world, without knowing my viewpoints. How would they know anything about me if they ask me without seeing half of me rather than the full access to me. I'm like Disney Plus for that matter, sign up for free but I'm on Premier Access, so you would have to pay $29.99, so about thirty bucks to get the full access in learning about me. Signing up onto Disney Plus is as easy as being forced to be friends with someone like me but unlocking me to get to know more about me is also like unlocking the Premier Access, to find the person I'm not expected to be.

It doesn't really occur to a neurotypical that we can be on the driver's seat of the car, not just the passenger's seat, not the back, the driver's seat. That is pretty F*ing simple, but so, so easy to forget that we neurodivergents are human beings just living our own lives trying to fit into society's precious little puzzle peg that is the shape of a star. That it has been long enough that we have to gingerly step, to gingerly walk around society's status quos, so we don't have to make a scene, to have to give in rather than to be accommodated in order to fit in. Like what Dr. Seuss once said, "why fit in when you were born to stand out?" Yes, why the heck would I fit in whenever I'm born to stand out, to have the privilege to be able to voice my opinion, to tell my own story and to control my own narrative, so I don't feel as if I'm being written out. And this was also one of the reasons why I've decided to write this book to tell things from my own point of view and as a neurodiverse being, not only to detect a difference between being neurotypicals and being neurodiverse, but to also to detect how a neuro-diverse feels in comparison.

    I'm born a human being; I'm born with a brain that feels and seems different than the rest. One peculiar thing is how we neurodiverse don't easily detect, don't sniff out bad people, our radars are missing that. But, hey, we aren't a different human species, we aren't aliens after all. I'm not an alien and I don't want to be treated as such, as if I couldn't take any curve balls thrown at me. I don't really need to be spoon-fed or to be coddled, holding the crown on my head as if I'm some rare Chinese plate. But there is a difference between being coddled and having someone to help you. Being coddled is something one does to another person, helps that person who can't digest the real truth or needs help with a revelation. I do understand those that can't really take on anything new, protecting those that can't handle it.

    This book is to tell my story in a point of view that may seem limited but it's adding another depth to what autism really means and adding to my own struggles along with the small victories in my life, which would make a rawer, a more real, and a more real story instead of just making it painfully glossy and sugar-coated. And well, it is about time for me to wrap up this book, but I don't really believe in the concept of 'happily ever after'. I do believe that there's another winding, rocky road ahead of me, waiting for me to walk on, waiting to walk onto the next phrase, the next chapter of my life. It has been a privilege.

    And I live optimistically happier than ever . . .

## EPILOGUE: "LIKE A POST-CREDIT SCENE"

Hello there . . . Woah, uh, wh-what . . . You're still here?!
You're still reading this? This book ends here, it's over, close the book already. Go. Wait not yet ~

Oh, wait, there's only one last thing to clarify. It's the utmost privilege to write this book, in the viewpoint of such as myself, instead of a file report from a hospital that first diagnosed me as autistic.

The ultimate goal, again, of this book is to spread awareness not for acceptance but to be aware of how we neurodiverse human beings are in fact humans; we just have different mindsets from the rest. We aren't a linear pathway to what the autism spectrum is or what it apparently supposed to be, in society's viewpoint in what they want it to be. Over the years, I've always thought that society often looks down, and frowns upon autistic people, but in hindsight, I've realized so slowly that people who aren't on the spectrum don't really know how to interact with people on said spectrum, they're uneasy about it and they don't know how to talk to people on the spectrum, as if we are from a totally different planet.

It's not a bad thing that society often doesn't

know how they could interact with people like me, because as I said we aren't the same as the rest. A strain of different personalities within the same spectrum.

We all have things we are very insecure about, neurotypical and neuro-diverse alike, we are creatures of habit with things that make us special and originary (original and ordinary). That also has a double meaning, clouding up our cerebellums like in a horror movie-type setting. But eventually the sun comes out from the clouds, to better understand internally, knowing from the inside out, you're exceptional. Sometimes, we got to run up that solid, brick wall in order to see the other side of that wall.

Somehow, I do feel conflicted by ending this book, like wrapping up a perfectly good, well-crafted biopic, to perfectly sum up the 'and he lived happily ever after' but does it really sum up after the *ever after*? Conflicted in how just a simple dramatic ending of my writing, me standing at a beautiful, open field, with the wind in my face and a predictable sunset in front, feeling as if I'm the only man in the world. Let's hope there are no joggers or bikers or even runners as bystanders who would be all like 'wtf he's doing?', that'll be like walking into someone who is in the middle of making a TikTok video. Or if I could drive, I'd be driving off to the sunset. To be clear, why is it always a sunset? Why can it be midday or at night, but no, it clearly has to be a sunset to perfectly wrap this sh*t up! And second of all, where the F I'm driving to?! Onto some highway or on some backroad with trees dramatically passing by like they are cartoonishly waving.

There are no good ways to simply and properly ending, wrapping this book. No cheesy lines that could've been on a wrapper of a Dove chocolate piece, or a fortune cookie. No fancy ways into doing so because the journey just begun; the sunsets symbols in what is to come upon me, no 'and he lived happily ever after, driving off, walking off, just staring off the blinding sunset'. But, in how I symbolize the sunset in anticipation of what is to come in the near, or distant future of my own beholding.

In fear, we hold back, and in fearlessness, we excel forward.

And also, just to keep in mind that everyone and anyone won't be able to understand your journey nor always think it has no meaning; it's somewhat meaningless. Don't let them think so cynical, so spiteful as a George Carlin comic bit about your life and your journeys and your choices in life. Just focus on to live the now, the journeys, and have the pens, typewriter, or computer, or whatever the F ready to tell your life's story so it feels truthful, honest, bold and unapologetic.

Yet again, in fear, we for sure hold back, and

in fearlessness, we for sure and definitely, we excel forward.

If you want to hear more about my journey, follow me on Instagram or TikTok.